Contents

1 BRITAIN IN 1500

Today we live in a country called the *United Kingdom of Great Britain and Northern Ireland.* Wales, Scotland, Northern Ireland and England are all different parts of the same country. This was not how things were in the year 1500. Britain in 1500 was very different to Britain today. Look at the map to see what it was like then.

OUT OF THE MIDDLE AGES

In the years since the Norman Conquest in 1066, there had been many changes in Britain. The people around the map remind us about some of the ones that made Britain what it was like in 1500.

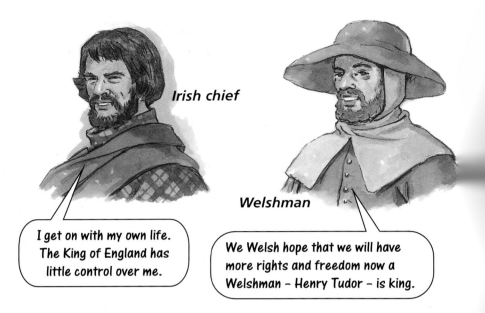

Irish chief

I get on with my own life. The King of England has little control over me.

Welshman

We Welsh hope that we will have more rights and freedom now a Welshman – Henry Tudor – is king.

NEW WORDS

CATHOLIC: the name for members of the Christian Church in most of Europe.

POPE: the leader of the Catholic Church. He lived in Rome.

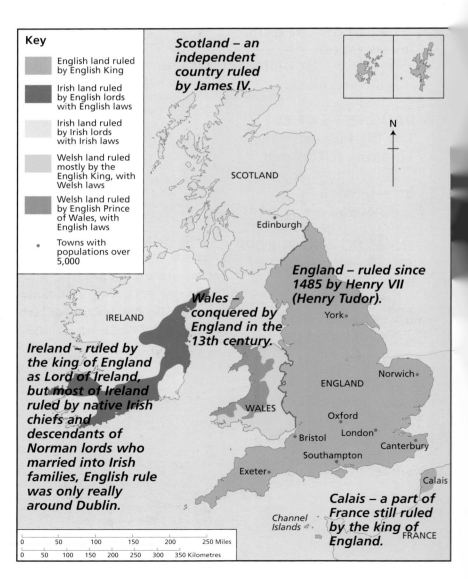

Key

- English land ruled by English King
- Irish land ruled by English lords with English laws
- Irish land ruled by Irish lords with Irish laws
- Welsh land ruled mostly by the English King, with Welsh laws
- Welsh land ruled by English Prince of Wales, with English laws
- Towns with populations over 5,000

Scotland – an independent country ruled by James IV.

SCOTLAND

Edinburgh

England – ruled since 1485 by Henry VII (Henry Tudor).

IRELAND

Wales – conquered by England in the 13th century.

York

Ireland – ruled by the king of England as Lord of Ireland, but most of Ireland ruled by native Irish chiefs and descendants of Norman lords who married into Irish families, English rule was only really around Dublin.

WALES

ENGLAND

Norwich

Oxford

Bristol

London

Southampton

Canterbury

Exeter

Calais

Calais – a part of France still ruled by the king of England.

Channel Islands

FRANCE

| 0 | 50 | 100 | 150 | 200 | 250 Miles |
| 0 | 50 | 100 | 150 | 200 | 250 | 300 | 350 Kilometres |

HODDER HISTORY

Cro
& C

Britain

MARTYN WHITTOCK

Acknowledgements

The front cover shows the execution of Charles I by an unknown artist reproduced courtesy of of the Earl of Rosebery / Scottish National Portrait Gallery, and Oliver Cromwell by Robert Walker reproduced courtesy of of the National Portrait Gallery, London.

The publishers would like to thank the following individuals, institutions and companies for permission to reproduce copyright illustrations in this book:
Henry VIII of England meeting Francis I of France on the Camp du Drap d'Or by Friedrich Bouterwerk, Musee du Chateau, Versailles/AKG Photo, London/VISIOARS page 6; Pope Alexander VI by Pinturicchio, Rome, Vatican, Appartamento Borgia/AKG Photo, London page13; Lord Cobham and his Family, 1567 by William Brooke/The Bridgeman Art Library/Longleat House, Wiltshire page 20 (Source A); The Tichborne Dole, 1670 by Gillis van Tilborg/The Bridgeman Art Library/Tichborne Park, Hampshire page 20 (Source B); Robert Gwillym of Atherton and his Family, c. 1745-7 by A Devis/The Bridgeman Art Library/Yale Centre for British Art, Paul Melon Collection, USA page 20 (Source C); Elizabeth I, Armada Portrait attr. to George Gower/The Bridgeman Art Library/Woburn Abby, Bedfordshire page 33 (Source C); The British Library pages 5, 34 (De Leone Belgico by Michael von Eyezingen, 1585); The British Museum pages 11 (left), 31 (middle); The Duke of Buccleuch and Queensbury, KT page 28; Corbis page 57 (bottom right); English Heritage Photo Library pages14, 20 (Source D), 21 (Source G); The Fotomas Index (UK) pages 19, 23 (Sources D and E), 24, 25 (Sources C, D and E), 43, 49, 50, 55, 57 (bottom left), 62; Marquess of Salisbury/The Fotomas Index (UK) pages 32, 33 (Source B); The Museum of London page 10; The National Maritime Museum page 38; The National Museums & Galleries on Merseyside pages 7, 33 (top left); National Museums & Galleries of Wales page 31; The National Portrait Gallery, London pages 4 (Henry VII by M Sittow, 1505), 26 and 27 (Sir Henry Unton, Soldier & Diplomat with scenes from his life by unknown artist c. 1596), 31 (top right), 31 (bottom) (Queen Anne by Sir Godfrey Kneller), 57 (top left) (William Harvey by unknown artist c. 1627) top right, Sir Isaac Newton by Sir Godfrey Kneller, 1702); National Trust Photographic Library page 21 (Source E, Rupert Truman), (Source F, Matthew Antrobus), (Sources H and I, Andreas von Einsiedel); The National Trust for Scotland page 66; Peter Lowry Photography page 17; Pepys Library, Magdalene College, Cambridge (PL 2973/447) page 63; Private Collections pages 51, 60; Readers Digest/Ivan Lapper page 18; The Cholmondeley Ladies, British School, 17th Century, Tate Picture Library page 29; Ulster Museum, Belfast page 39; Robert Boyle engraving by J Chapman/The Trustee of the Wellcome Trust, London page 57 (top middle), Wellcome Institute Library, London page 59; The Worshipful Company of Goldsmiths page 11 (right).

The publishers would also like to thank the following for permission to reproduce material in this book:
Blackwell Publishers for the extract from *They Saw It Happen Vol II* by CRN Routh, Basil Blackwell, 1956; James P Carley for the extracts from *Glastonbury Abbey* by JP Carley, Boydell & Brewer Ltd, 1988; Curtis Brown for the extracts from *Tudor England* by John Guy, OUP, 1988; Macmillan Press Ltd for extracts from *The Age of Expansion* by L Smith, 1986; © Ronald Hutton 1996, *Stations of the Sun: A History of the Ritual Year in Britain* by Ronald Hutton (1996), by permission of Oxford University Press; Stanley Thornes (Publishers) Ltd for the extract from *A World of Change* by R Kelly, 1987.

The publishers would like to acknowledge the use of material from the BBC TV History File.

Please note that some sources have been adapted to make them more accessible to students.

Every effort has been made to trace and acknowledge ownership of copyright. The publishers will be glad to make suitable arrangements with any copyright holders whom it has not been possible to contact.

My special thanks to Hannah Whittock for assistance with historical research and checking the text and to Esther Whittock for artwork advice.

To John, Ruth, Bethanna, Joseph and Samuel Chettleburgh, in thanks for their friendship.

Orders: please contact Bookpoint Ltd, 130 Milton Park, Abingdon, Oxon OX14 4SB. Telephone: (44) 01235 827720, Fax: (44) 01235 400454. Lines are open from 9.00 - 6.00, Monday to Saturday, with a 24 hour message answering service. You can also order through our website at www.hodderheadline.co.uk

British Library Cataloguing in Publication Data
A catalogue record for this title is available from The British Library

ISBN 0 340 75344 7

First published 2000
Impression number   10 9 8 7 6
Year   2005 2004

Copyright © 2000 Martyn Whittock

Typeset by Liz Rowe.
Printed in Italy for Hodder & Stoughton Educational, a division of Hodder Headline, 338 Euston Road, London NW1 3BH.

We nobles are rich and powerful. We'll do what we can to make sure the King rules in the way we like.

Nobleman

Scotsman

We Scots don't trust our old enemies the English. We'll work with the enemies of England to keep the English out of Scotland.

We are rediscovering the ideas of the ancient Greeks and Romans about art, science, architecture and government. New printed books spread these ideas. Some of us think the Church should be changed to make it holier and more like it was when it started. We are challenging lots of old ways of doing things!

University student

We are a Christian people. The Church is powerful and rich. It is loved and respected and brings people close to God. We are part of the great **Catholic** Church and the **Pope** in Rome has been made head of the Church by God.

Churchman

The King must get the agreement of Parliament if he wants new taxes. You can't ignore Parliament!

Member of Parliament

Q **1.** Design a Tourist Board poster to encourage people to visit 'Britain 1500'. On your poster mention:
- How many countries there are in 'Britain 1500'.
- Who rules them.
- An overview of how some of the people living there feel about life.

2. Look at the information about Britain on the map. In what ways is Britain today different to Britain in 1500? Which do you think is the most important difference and why?

2 THE TUDOR KINGS

THIS CHAPTER ASKS
Who were the Tudors?
How well did Henry VII rule?
How great a king was Henry VIII?

NEW WORDS

NOBLE: a rich and powerful landowner.

WHO WAS HENRY VII?

Henry Tudor became King Henry VII of England in 1485. In that year his army defeated King Richard III at the Battle of Bosworth. Legend says that Richard's crown was found hanging on a thorn bush and placed on Henry's head. During the fifteenth century two branches of the royal family had fought for the right to rule. These were the Lancastrians and the Yorkists. The wars they fought were the 'Wars of the Roses'. Richard III was a Yorkist and Henry was a Lancastrian. Henry did not have a very strong claim to the throne. His grandfather had married the widow of the Lancastrian King Henry V. After he had killed Richard III in battle and become king, he faced a lot of problems:

- There was terrible rivalry between the families of York and Lancaster.
- Powerful **nobles** were trying to control him.
- He was very short of money.
- He needed peace with foreign countries.

Henry VII was the first Welsh person to become ruler of England. On his coat of arms was the red dragon of Wales.

A TOUGH AND CAREFUL KING

Once he felt in control of the country, Henry married Princess Elizabeth, daughter of the dead Yorkist King Edward IV. This united the two rival halves of the royal family.

Henry knew that during the fifteenth century many nobles had become independent and powerful. He was determined to bring them under his control. He forced them to promise to be loyal and fined them if they disobeyed him. Out of 62 noble families, only 16 escaped having to sign one of these agreements with the king. He forced many to loan him money and hunted out anyone who owed him money.

SOURCE A

A portrait of Henry VII painted in 1505. ▶

CRUSHING REVOLTS

Henry was determined not to be overthrown. He made sure that castles were put under the control of trusted friends. He was ready to crush any revolts. In 1487 the Yorkists organised a revolt, pretending that a young man named Lambert Simnel was Earl of Warwick and should be king. The revolt was crushed but Henry forgave Lambert and gave him a job in the royal kitchens! In 1497 Henry crushed another Yorkist revolt. In this revolt Perkin Warbeck pretended to be one of the murdered sons of the Yorkist King Edward IV. He was helped by the kings of Scotland and France who were enemies of England. Henry had Perkin executed and made peace with Scotland and France.

SOURCE B

The king, not wanting to make poor people pay for his soldiers, took money only from the rich. Henry in this copied King Edward IV. This allowed him to tell how much a person loved him, something he had not been able to check on before.

▲ *Written by an Italian visitor to England, Polydore Vergil, who lived during Henry VII's reign.*

SOURCE C

◄ *A picture of Henry VII's counting house where his servants checked who owed him money.*

HENRY AND PARLIAMENT

Henry VII ran the country using the help and advice of his most trusted nobles. These made up his Council. Sometimes he called in other nobles and leading townspeople to form a Great Council.

He did not allow Parliament to have much power. In fact in a period of 23 years and eight months, Parliament only met for 72 weeks! Its job was to agree to new taxes, not to tell the king how to run the country! Henry was determined to hold power himself.

Q

1. Make a spidergram to illustrate the problems Henry VII faced when he became king. Then draw an arrow out from each of these problems and by its end explain what Henry did to try to solve these problems.

2. Look carefully at your diagram. How well did Henry tackle his problems?

3. How can **Source B** be used to show that Henry tried to solve different problems with one action?

HENRY VIII

Henry VII's eldest son – Arthur – died, and so, when Henry VII himself died in 1509, he was succeeded by his second son. Also named Henry, he became King Henry VIII.

HENRY THE GREAT?

Henry is one of the most famous kings in English History. Henry was 'big' in many ways: he had six wives; he owned 55 palaces, 2000 tapestries, almost 2,000 books and 94 swords; he executed two wives and 12 nobles; he destroyed 563 monasteries and made himself Head of the Church of England. No wonder people remember Henry! He was not the kind of person you forgot in a hurry. As a young king he was intelligent, handsome and sporty. By the time he died in 1547 he was massively overweight, trusted no one, was easily annoyed and was a very dangerous man to fall out with. But was he a great king?

SOURCE A

Henry VIII built and collected more than any other English king. He also demolished, destroyed and got rid of more. The cost in people and things was immense. But in his day magnificence in peace and glory in war were thought to be what kings were about.

▲ *Written by the modern historian, David Starkey, in* **Henry VIII, A European Court in England,** *1991.*

SOURCE B

▲ *In 1520 Henry met King Francis I of France. They met in France. Henry put on a huge show to impress Francis. A temporary palace was built for Henry, there was feasting and tournaments, there was even a huge English firework in the shape of a great dragon. It was called The Field of the Cloth of Gold.*

HENRY'S SUCCESSES

Henry wanted to unite the country and make it powerful. In 1536 he made Wales fully part of England, and in 1541 he took the title King of Ireland to show he was determined to control it. Henry defended the south coast of England by building defences that were not matched until the 20th century. He spent money on ships such as the *Mary Rose*. His daughter, Elizabeth I, was able to beat the Spanish Armada in 1588 partly due to the fact that Henry had put so much money into warships. He spent huge amounts of money to make his court respected and admired by people in this country and abroad. He seemed a great king.

HENRY'S PROBLEMS

Henry spent vast amounts of money on wars and on weapons. He wanted everyone to think he was powerful but he could not really afford it. Because of this, less and less silver was put into English coins to save money. When these coins were used the silver wore off on the portrait of the king's head. Underneath, the metal was copper coloured, not silver. Soon one of Henry's nicknames amongst ordinary people was 'old coppernose'.

Henry wanted to be a warrior king. Within two years of the Field of the Cloth of Gold, England was once again at war with France. But Henry could not win. France was three times as large as England and Wales, and had a population five times bigger. Henry was clever enough, though, to make peace and appear stronger than he really was. But he was frustrated against the Scots. He won a huge victory over them at Solway Moss, in 1542, but could never manage to crush them. To make matters worse, the French gave them help.

DIVORCED, BEHEADED, DIED, DIVORCED, BEHEADED, SURVIVED

This is what happened to Henry's wives – Catherine of Aragon, Anne Boleyn, Jane Seymour, Catherine Howard, Anne of Cleves and Catherine Parr. Henry was desperate to have a son. But the son he had by Jane was sickly and, in the end, it was his daughters Mary and Elizabeth who became famous rulers. All three had to cope with a country heavily taxed and short of money because of Henry's spending.

SOURCE C

▲ *One of the most famous portraits of King Henry VIII. It was painted by Holbein who knew Henry well.*

While Henry's body was lying in its coffin at Syon Abbey, waiting to be buried, it rotted so much it exploded. The coffin burst open and blood, fat and rotting bits sprayed all over the floor.

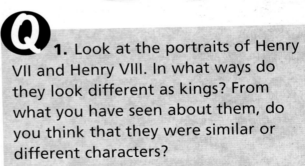

Q 1. Look at the portraits of Henry VII and Henry VIII. In what ways do they look different as kings? From what you have seen about them, do you think that they were similar or different characters?

2. How successful a king was Henry VIII?
■ Mention the problems he faced.
■ His successes.
■ His failures.
■ Your overall conclusion.

3. From what you have learned about Henry VII and Henry VIII, who do you think was the more successful king? Explain why you think so.

Why did Thomas Cromwell fall?

A DEADLY GAME

Henry worked through trusted servants who planned and carried out his wishes. But Henry was a dangerous man to serve. Any failure could cost a man his life and no one was allowed to disagree with the king. On top of this, powerful groups at court were always competing to try to influence the king and use the power he gave those he trusted. They were always keen to point out to Henry any mistakes made by their rivals. Life at court could be a deadly game.

Three of Henry's trusted servants were **Cardinal** Wolsey, Sir Thomas More and Thomas Cromwell. All were eventually destroyed because they fell out with Henry. Wolsey was a hard-working man who ran both the English Church and government. It was said at the time that he would work for 12 hours non-stop, to sort out problems for the king, without a meal or a visit to the toilet! But when he failed to get Henry's divorce from his first wife, Catherine, Henry stripped him of his power – he died in disgrace in 1530.

Thomas More let it be known he thought it wrong that Henry had made himself Head of the English Church instead of the pope. So Henry had him executed. And then there was Thomas Cromwell...

NEW WORDS

CARDINAL: a very high ranking person in the Catholic Church.
MONASTERIES: places where monks and nuns live and worship God, separated from the opposite sex and away from the world.
PROTESTANTS: Christians who do not believe that the Catholic pope is head of the Church. They believe that only the Bible should be used to find out what is right and wrong.

1 1514 Cromwell began to work for Henry's chief minister, Wolsey.

2 Ruthless at getting things done. Feared by many but liked by Wolsey who made him his secretary.

6 1536 began shutting down monasteries. Their wealth went to Henry.

7 1539 had Bible translated from Latin into English. Protestants pleased. Henry not happy about this.

SOURCE A

He was the hammer of the monks and a brave soldier and Captain fighting for Christ.

▲ *Written by John Foxe, a 16th-century English writer who wanted the Church in England to be changed from Catholic to Protestant.*

SOURCE B

I did not like her much before but now I like her even less ... she looks like a Flander's mare.

▲ *Henry VIII's opinion of his new wife, Anne of Cleves. Flanders is in Europe and a mare is a female horse.*

Q

1. Look at **Source A**. Why might a historian feel that this writer's opinion of Cromwell might not say all we need to know about the kind of man he was?

2. Look at **Source B**. Do you think this was Henry's only reason for turning against Cromwell?

3. Imagine you are a priest sent to hear Cromwell's confession before he died. What might he have told you about:

■ How and why he became so useful to Wolsey and Henry.

■ The reasons why he fell from power?

When Wolsey fell, the king took on Cromwell and gave him many powerful jobs.

1534 helped Henry divorce Catherine of Aragon.

Helped Henry become Head of the Church in England.

1540 arranged marriage between Henry and Anne of Cleves. Henry did not like her.

Cromwell's enemies said he was changing the Church more than he should. Cromwell executed.

It's the thought that counts!

YOUR MISSION: to buy the right gift for Henry VIII.

It is New Year's Day, 1538, and King Henry VIII is meeting his court in the great **Presence Chamber** of Greenwich Palace, near London. In the 16th century, New Year's Day, not Christmas Day, was the great gift-giving day. On this day the members of the court gave a present to the king and in return got a present from him. You are a noble having to choose a gift for the king. If he likes your present, you might get a really big present back! The king usually gives golden plates, cups and jugs, so his present could be worth a lot of money to you.

But first you need to get him a present that will really impress him. But what does he like?

- Rich and beautiful items
- Things that show a lot of skill in their workmanship
- Fashionable things
- Clever things that combine different ideas, or uses

Remember, if the king likes your gift, you'll get a rich gift in return and maybe he will remember you when he's got a good job that needs doing. That's how it works at court!

NEW WORDS

PLATE Objects made of gold or silver.

PRESENCE CHAMBER: Place in the palace where the King met people.

SOURCE A

In the Tudor and Stuart periods, New Year gifts united relationships at the heart of the government. From the ruler gold or silver **plate** was given in fixed amounts, from the 136 ounces given to a favourite, to 2 ounces received by the court dwarf. In return, the ruler was given rich clothing, money, jewels and other presents, down to the marzipan sent by the cook!

▲ *Written by a modern historian, Ronald Hutton, in* **The Stations of the Sun**, *1997.*

SOURCE B

◄ *A fashionable jug made by an Italian craftsperson. It is expensive. You would have to borrow some money to buy it.*

SOURCE **C**

When I entered the Presence Chamber to present Lord Lisle's gift, Cromwell smiled and said to the king, 'Here comes my Lord Lisle's man'. The king said 'I thank my lord. How are my lord and my lady? Are they merry?' The king stood by the cupboard, receiving all things and Mr Tuke (a secretary) wrote down all the things that were given.

▲ *John Hussey recalls how he presented the New Year's gift of his lord, Viscount Lisle, to King Henry VIII in 1538. Viscount Lisle could not be there because he was in charge of English soldiers in Calais, the town the English ruled in France.*

SOURCE **E**

▲ *A handful of valuable gold coins. You could afford to give these to the king.*

SOURCE **D**

▲ *A magnificent clock which is also a container for salt. At the bottom are little pictures called cameos which were very fashionable. You would have to borrow a great deal of money to be able to give this to the king.*

INVESTIGATION

You are the investigator!

You are a noble. What gift would you buy King Henry VIII? Which of **Sources B, D** and **E** would you give him?

■ Describe what he likes.

■ Explain why gift giving is so important at the Tudor court.

■ Write down the arguments for and against giving each of these gifts.

Then make your final decision.

■ Explain why you have chosen this gift and why you think it is better than the other ones. Do you have any worries about your choice?

3 CHANGES IN THE CHURCH

THIS CHAPTER ASKS

Why was the 16th-century Catholic church facing change?

Why did Henry VIII fall out with the pope?

How much did the Church in England change under the Tudors?

Why did Henry VIII destroy the monasteries?

NEW WORDS

RELIC: something belonging to a holy person.

SIN: wrong-doing that sends a person to hell.

SUPERSTITION: believing in something that does not really exist.

Do you go to a church? Or to a synagogue, or mosque, or mandira? Today, while more people in Britain are members of the Christian Church than any other religion, this country is a multi-faith society, in which many different religious groups live together. This was not how things were in the 16th century. Then, almost everyone in Britain was a Christian. Today, amongst Christians there are different groups or denominations. A Christian might be a member of the Church of England, or a Methodist, a Baptist, a Pentecostal, or another group. They all believe Jesus is the Son of God but have different ideas about things like how a church should be run, how services should be organised.

In the 16th century every Christian in Britain was a member of the same church, which included every Christian in western Europe. It was called the Catholic Church and its leader, the pope, lived in Rome. This Church was very powerful. Over the centuries it had been given property and land and was very wealthy. In addition to this, the pope claimed that God had given him the authority to decide what Christians could and could not do, what was right and wrong. Catholic people believed that if they lived the way the Church taught and obeyed the pope they would go to heaven when they died. People were afraid to disagree with the pope because they thought this would make God angry. They thought that this would mean they would be sent to hell when they died. But things were changing.

Henry said he should divorce Catherine because it was wrong to have sex with a woman who had been married to his brother. But Henry married Anne despite the fact he had had sex with her sister, Mary!

CHANGING TIMES

In the 16th century the Catholic Church was facing many challenges to its power.

- Many rulers resented a foreigner, the pope, having power over people in their country;
- Many educated people disagreed with the way the Church tried to control ideas and education. Their ideas were spread by a new invention – printing;
- Some within the Church said the popes were too rich and corrupt and should live holier lives;
- Some preachers said the only things Christians should believe in were what was in the Bible.

SOURCE A

The king our sovereign lord, his heirs and successors kings of this realm shall be taken as the only supreme head on earth of the Church of England

▲ *The words of the Act of Supremacy, 1534. Another law that year meant anyone who disagreed with this could be executed for treason.*

THE REFORMATION AND PROTESTANTS

In 1517 a German monk, Martin Luther, said Christians should believe the Bible not the pope. He thought it wrong that the Catholic Church said people could buy forgiveness for their **sins** and treated **relics** as if they were holy.

Later, historians were to call what Luther started *The Reformation*. By the end of the 16th century it had split the Catholic Church. Those who believed in the old way of doing things remained Catholics. Those who wanted change became *Protestants*. Protestants did not agree about everything, but there were certain things they did agree about:

■ The Bible told people about God; people should be able to read the Bible in their own language not in Latin, which Catholics preferred.

■ People would get to heaven only by trusting in Jesus forgiving them, not by doing good things.

■ People could pray straight to God and not rely on saints or the Virgin Mary to speak to God for them.

■ Bones of saints (relics) were not holy and trusting in them to work a miracle was just **superstition**.

■ Churches should be simpler and not so ornate.

HENRY VIII FALLS OUT WITH THE POPE

Henry was not a Protestant. In fact the pope gave him the title 'Defender of the Faith' because he had a book written attacking Protestant ideas. But Henry was desperate for a son, and his wife, Catherine of Aragon, had not produced one. He wanted to divorce her and marry another woman, Anne Boleyn, and by December 1532 Anne was pregnant. The pope would not agree to Henry divorcing Catherine. Henry broke with the pope, made himself Head of the Church in England and made sure the leaders of the English Church agreed with his divorce and remarriage to Anne Boleyn. But in 1533 Anne had a girl – the future Queen Elizabeth I. Henry's plan had failed.

▲ *A painting of Pope Alexander VI (1492–1503). Like many popes, he was a rich and powerful ruler. Many people in the 16th century thought that popes should live simpler and holier lives.*

Q

1. Carry out a survey in your class of who has gone to a place of religious worship in the last week. If you had carried out the same survey in 1530, do you think you would have had the same results? Explain your answer.

2. Imagine you were one of the early Protestants and design a protest poster, complaining about the way the Catholic Church is run and suggesting ways it could be improved.

3. If you had been pope in 1533, who would you have thought was the greatest threat to the Catholic Church – Luther or Henry VIII? Explain the reasons for your choice.

THE CHURCH UNDER HENRY VIII

In 1532 Henry forced the priests to accept that he controlled the English Church. This became law in 1534 and he became 'Supreme Head' of the English Church. In 1536 another law ended the power of the pope in England. In 1536 Henry's servant Cromwell began 'dissolving' (destroying) monasteries in England. This removed people who were still Catholic and Henry wanted their lands and property.

THE BIG PICTURE

NEW WORDS

CELIBATE: unmarried.
MASS: communion. Catholics believe the bread and wine become the body and blood of Jesus. Protestants do not.
ROOD LOFTS: balconies on which there were crosses and statues of saints.

SOURCE A

◄ *When Henry destroyed the monasteries their buildings were wrecked. This is Roche Abbey, in Yorkshire.*

In 1536 there were Catholic revolts in the north, known as 'the Pilgrimage of Grace'. They were crushed. English Bibles replaced Latin ones and priests were encouraged to do more preaching. But Henry was not a Protestant – he wanted a Catholic Church under his control and with a few changes.

REVOLUTION – KING EDWARD VI

When Henry died, in 1547, the service of **mass** was still the main church service, people still prayed to saints, holy relics still existed, priests remained **celibate** and prayers were prayed for the dead. This was all very Catholic.

Under Henry's son, Edward VI, this all changed. Statues of saints were destroyed after 1548. In 1549, an English Prayer Book replaced the Latin services. In 1552, priests were allowed to marry. Communion tables replaced stone altars in churches. Priests wore less ornate robes.

AND BACK AGAIN – QUEEN MARY TUDOR

When Edward died, in 1553, his Catholic half-sister, Mary, became queen. She brought back Catholic bishops. Priests could no longer marry, statues, altars and **rood lofts** went back up in churches. Priests wore more ornate robes. Mary burned 287 Protestants.

COMPROMISE – QUEEN ELIZABETH I

When Mary died, in 1558, her half-sister, Elizabeth, became queen. Elizabeth was a Protestant but wanted the country peaceful. Statues, relics, altars and fancy priest's robes were destroyed. But it was harder for priests to marry, they wore some formal clothes, some churches kept their altars and kneeling and bowing was allowed in church services. Some people – soon to be called Puritans – thought Elizabeth was not going far enough to make England Protestant.

Not everyone liked the changes to the Church. In 1565 parishes around Coventry were ordered to choose up to eight 'bouncers' for each church, to stop protests during church services and throw out trouble-makers.

Q **1.** Look at the two churches. Explain what is similar, and what is different about them.

2. Imagine you are a priest in the period between 1546 and 1580. Explain how the church has changed:

■ who is in charge;

■ types of services;

■ changes to church buildings;

■ changes to your life.

You can tell how you feel from either a Catholic or a Protestant point of view.

Death at Glastonbury

YOUR MISSION: to find out why the Abbot of Glastonbury was hanged.

It was 15 November 1539, a cold and windy autumn day. The **Abbot** of Glastonbury, Richard Whiting – old and ill – was dragged to the top of the Tor, the high hill beside the town of Glastonbury. Bravely he waited for death; beside him were two other monks, also condemned to die. There, Whiting and the other monks were hanged. Afterwards the old man's head was chopped off and his body hacked into four parts. Each part was sent to a nearby Somerset town – Bath, Wells, Ilchester and Bridgewater. His head was placed over the gateway of his abbey. But Henry VIII's men had already stripped everything of value from it.

One more abbey had been destroyed and its riches taken by the king. But why did Whiting die?

NEW WORDS

ABBOT: the monk in charge of a monastery.

DICE: gambling, usually for money.

SOURCE A

Whiting was a truly good man and his character was spotless and he was my good friend.

▲ *Written by the 16th-century traveller, John Leland, who knew and visited Glastonbury. Leland usually did not like monks and abbots.*

The nursery rhyme Little Jack Horner is actually about how John Horner was sold a 'plumb' – the manor of Mells – by King Henry VIII.

SOURCE B

Whiting never really believed in God. Not when I first met him nor now. He is not loyal to the king and knows nothing about how to be a real Christian. I cannot be sure of my views to know what he is like inside but careful checking shows he is fine outside and rotten inside.

▲ *Written in 1539 by Richard Layton, one of the king's servants, who visited monasteries to destroy them. In 1535 Layton had written that Whiting was a good man. But in 1539 he was sent back to catch Whiting out and destroy the abbey.*

SOURCE C

'The abbot does not give me food for my family when they visit.'
'The beer tastes bad.'
'The abbot spends money on himself that should be spent on all of us.'
'We are badly taught and have little to do but play at **dice** and cards.'
'Services are long and boring and there is not enough time left to study.'

▲ *Complaints made about the abbot and the abbey by Glastonbury monks when the Bishop of Bath and Wells visited the abbey in 1538. The purpose of his visit was to discover complaints.*

Photograph of the manor house at Mells in Somerset. It belonged to Glastonbury Abbey, but after the death of Abbot Whiting, it was bought by John Horner, a supporter of the king. ➤

SOURCE E

SOURCE D

It is the best abbey that we have ever seen. A house good enough for the king himself and for no one else. The abbey is great, fine and so royal that we have never seen anything like it. It has four parks nearby, a great lake well stocked with fish. The abbot owns four fine manor houses. The furthest is only three miles away.

⬆ **Letter written in 1539 to Thomas Cromwell from the royal officials sent to examine Glastonbury Abbey.**

SOURCE G

I know of nothing found which puts him in the wrong except a book disagreeing with the king's divorce [from Catherine of Aragon].

⬆ **Written by the French ambassador, Charles de Marillac, in October 1539, about the evidence against Abbot Whiting.**

SOURCE H

The abbot of Glastonbury is to be sent down to be tried and then executed at Glastonbury.

⬆ **Written by Thomas Cromwell, November 1539. He assumes that Whiting will be found guilty even before his trial.**

SOURCE F

He was broken hearted and just an old, weak and sick man. We demanded that he remember what he had forgotten and tell us the truth. We searched and found a letter written against the king's divorce, which we think is very serious. We are sure the abbot has the rotten heart of a traitor.

⬆ **The report of the three royal officials who mercilessly questioned the sick Richard Whiting in September 1539.**

I NVESTIGATION

You are the investigator!

You are the agents of King Henry VIII sent to Glastonbury to make sure that Abbot Whiting is found guilty and his monastery given to the king. But how to do this?

■ Explain why the king might want Glastonbury;

■ List all the possible 'crimes' you might accuse the abbot of committing;

■ Choose the 'crime' likely to get him executed;

■ How will you deal with anyone who says the abbot is just a good, old, sick man and leave him alone?

17

4 TOWN AND COUNTRY

NEW WORDS

GENTLEMAN: a wealthy and respected person. In Tudor times this was decided by ownership of land not just how much money a person had.

PLAGUE: the disease bubonic plague.

THIS CHAPTER ASKS
What kind of country was Tudor England and Wales?
How did the rich live?
Why were the poor treated so badly?

LIFE IN TUDOR TOWNS

Only one out of every ten people in Tudor times lived in towns. These were often dirty and unhealthy places. In them there were often outbreaks of **plague** and other diseases like smallpox, influenza, and one that people at the time called 'the sweat' but is still a mystery to us today.

Towns could often be dangerous too – there were thieves, prostitutes and pickpockets. Streets were muddy and at night lacked lights. Many wealthy people were concerned at what they felt were the growing number of beggars.

Some of the people in towns became very rich but were often not thought of as 'gentlemen' because they did not own land. Many merchants, as well as craftspeople and shopkeepers, were looked down on by landowners even though they were actually quite well off!

In theory every craftsman in a town had the right to elect those who ran the town. But really towns were run by a small group of rich families who controlled the trade. These families were often related to each other. As well as deciding town business, they often chose the town's MP and ran the courts that tried criminals and settled disputes.

So why live in a town? It offered a choice of jobs, more freedom to make money, and entertainment such as the theatre. It was in towns that men like Shakespeare made their name. In a town there was always something to do!

SOURCE A

▲ *A modern artist's reconstruction painting of a Tudor street scene. To produce this the artist will have used documents from Tudor times such as court records, travellers accounts, and pictures drawn at the time.*

SOURCE B

A baby born in 1570 could expect to live on average for 38 years. Today the average life expectancy is about 74 years.

▲ *A picture of a country wedding at Bermondsey in 1592. Today Bermondsey is in the middle of London.*

A COUNTRY OF VILLAGES

Nine out of every ten people in Tudor times lived in the country. Farming became more efficient and there were very few famines compared to Medieval times. Tudor England was able to feed its people. Many historians think that, for all its problems, people in Tudor times were better off than at any time since the Romans.

The population, which had been about 2 million in 1450, rose to about 2.5 million in 1525, and in 1601 it reached about 4.1 million. People got married younger and had more babies. More of these babies survived to become adults themselves. As more people wanted more food, some farmers made a lot of money growing grain for bread. These better off farmers were called 'yeomen'. If they owned land worth 40 shillings a year they could even vote in elections to parliament. Above them were the 'gentry'.

But life in the countryside was still hard for the poor. In some areas landowners threw people off the land to make room for sheep, and in some areas the rent paid for land in 1640 was ten times as much as in 1510. The lives of unemployed people were made worse by the fact that prices were going up. In the 16th century the price of food went up 400 per cent. Not everyone could afford this.

Q

1. Look at **Source A**. Use this and the other evidence in this BIG PICTURE to explain the attractions of living in a Tudor town.

2. What were the disadvantages of town life?

3. 'Life in the country was hard.' Say whether you agree or disagree with this interpretation, and why.

Discussion Point
Why is there such a greater life expectancy today compared with 1570?

The life of the rich

CHANGING PLACES

For the rich, life was always more comfortable and healthier. The illustrations show wealthy families, homes and living rooms from three periods in English History: **Tudor**, **Stuart** and **Georgian**. Look carefully at the evidence and decide which people, houses and rooms belong together.

NEW WORDS

GEORGIAN: From George I to the death of George IV, 1714–1830
STUART: From James I to the death of Queen Anne, 1603–1714
TUDOR: From Henry VII to the death of Elizabeth I, 1485–1603.

SOURCE A

◀ *Lord Cobham and family, 1567.*

SOURCE B

◀ *Sir Henry Tichborne, family and servants, 1670.*

SOURCE C

▲ *Robert Gwillym and family, 1750.*

SOURCE D

▲ *Marble Hill House.*

SOURCE **E**

▲ *Little Moreton Hall, Cheshire.*

SOURCE **F**

Q **1.** Identify the people, house and rooms that you think are:

a. Tudor

b. Stuart

c. Georgian.

Then check your answers with your teacher.

2. Explain how life changed for the rich between 1500 and 1750. Mention fashion, house architecture, furniture and living styles. Did any things stay the same?

3. Which period of History would you have preferred to be rich in: Tudor, Stuart or Georgian? Why?

Discussion Point
How does wealth affect people's life chances today?

◄ *Nunnington Hall, Yorkshire.*

SOURCE **G**

▲ *Music room.*

SOURCE **H**

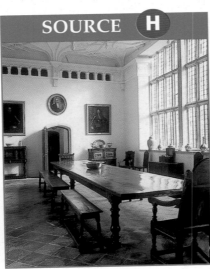

▲ *Hall.*

SOURCE **I**

▲ *Great hall.*

The beggars are coming

A DIVIDED COUNTRY?

In England today most people live very well – with cars, TVs, and comfortable houses – but some live on the streets and beg. And newspapers often speak more about what they call '**scroungers**' than the causes of poverty. This divide between rich and poor is shocking but not new.

During the 16th century the living standards of many people improved. Many farmers were able to sell their produce at higher prices than before and could afford to rebuild their farmhouses and live better. It's true that even for those less well off the fear of famine grew less as the more efficient farmers were able to produce more food and keep Tudor England well supplied.

But life is complicated. By 1600 there were more poor people than there had been in 1500. Why?

CAUSES OF TUDOR POVERTY

About two in every five people in Tudor England lived on the edge of poverty. It did not take much to push them under. During the 16th century prices went up. This '**inflation**' made it hard for some people to afford to live. Unemployment increased because of problems in the wool cloth industry. This hit some areas of the country badly.

NEW WORDS

IMPOTENT: unable to do something.

INFLATION: when prices rise and money buys less.

PAUPERS: poor people who were not to blame for their poverty.

SCROUNGERS: someone who is accused of being lazy and taking things from hard-working people.

SOURCE A

My father was a yeoman and had no land of his own. He had a farm costing three or four pounds' rent a year. Yet he could afford to keep me at school. But the farmer who now has the farm pays sixteen pounds a year and cannot afford to do anything for himself or his children.

▲ *Written in 1549 by Bishop Latimer. He came from a farming family and understood their problems.*

SOURCE B

How many cities that have declined, how many towns that have shrunk to hamlets would improve if a third of England did not live lazily?

▲ *Written in 1536 by Richard Moryson. He was worried about the cost of helping the poor.*

SOURCE C

If you look in any part of the country that grows the finest and dearest wool, there you find noblemen and even certain abbots have abused the public interest. They enclose land for sheep. They tear down houses and leave nothing standing but the church to be made into a sheep-house.

▲ *Written by Thomas More in 1516. He was a well-educated member of the government. He wanted old ways of life to be protected in the countryside.*

One judge from Kent claimed that in the 1520s a band of 280 beggars was found sheltering in one barn.

Some farmers threw people off their land to make room for sheep, which made more money. In the past the poor got help from monasteries but Henry VIII had shut these.

Rich people feared that the poor were lazy and might become criminals. They were particularly worried about 'sturdy beggars'. These were fit and healthy beggars that wandered from town to town. An official survey of 1569 found these made up only 0.4 per cent of the population but this did not stop rich people from panicking about the dangers of 'sturdy beggars'. Laws called Poor Laws were passed by parliament between 1531 and 1601. These gave help to the sick and old (the '**impotent** poor') and **paupers** wanting to find work, but for 'sturdy beggars' there were whippings and a hole burnt though one ear. In 1572 the death penalty was introduced for those caught begging twice. But Tudor writers could not always agree why poverty had increased.

SOURCE D

▲ *A picture of a Tudor harvest, 1510.*

SOURCE E

▲ *A country scene in 1540.*

Q

1. Look at **Sources D** and **E**.
a. What changes do these show as having happened in the countryside?
b. How might these changes have led to an increase in the number of poor people?
2. Using all the sources, make a spidergram to show the different Tudor suggestions as to why there was an increase in the numbers of poor people.
3. Which of these Tudor suggestions do you think was the most important reason?
4. Look at the information about the writers of **Sources A**, **B** and **C**. Which do you think is the most reliable? Which the least reliable? Explain how you decided.

Discussion Point
What should be done to help the homeless today?

23

A walk on the wild side

YOUR MISSION: to write a guide, 'How to stay alive in London', for a visitor to Elizabethan England.

London in the 16th century was busy and bustling but it could also be very dangerous. In its streets and alleyways there was an 'underworld' of criminals - thieves, muggers, murderers and prostitutes. It was a world of crime complete with its own secret language. Here is some of it:

autem – church	*beak* – judge	*bene* – good
bit – money	*booze* – drink	*bung* – purse
chats – **gallows**	*cony* – victim	*cove* – man
darkmans – night	*duds* – clothes	*flick* – thief
ken – house	*lift* – rob a shop	*mort* – woman
peck – food	*prancer* – horse	*queerken* – prison
stow you – shut up	*tip* – give	*yarrum* – milk

And there were so many cheats. An *angler* carried a pole to steal clothes. A *clapperdudgeon* put **arsenic** on his skin to make it bleed like a sore to make people pity him. A *Tom O'Bedlam* pretended to be mad. They were all out to con you, rob you, maybe even kill you! Could you stay alive?

NEW WORDS

ARSENIC: a poison.
BROTHEL: a house of prostitutes.
EPILEPTIC: a person with an illness that causes them to have fits and froth at the mouth.
GALLOWS: where criminals are hanged.
LOADED DICE: dice fixed to fall on certain numbers.
RAPIER: sword with a long, thin blade.

SOURCE A

▲ *A 16th-century picture of some of the criminals in London. These were called* baretop tricksters. *They met men and persuaded them to buy them a meal in a nearby* brothel. *The food cost a lot of money but the men were given sex too. Men who did this were often beaten up and robbed by gangs waiting for them.*

SOURCE B

Seldom shall you see any of my countrymen above the age of eighteen without at least a dagger in his belt or by his side. Our nobles usually wear swords or **rapiers** with their daggers, as does every common serving man that follows his lord and master.

▲ *Written in 1586 by William Harrison, in* A Description of England.

SOURCE C

▲ *16th-century picture of a gambling house. Gamblers were often cheated because loaded dice were used to make them lose.*

SOURCE D

▲ *A 16th-century picture of a pickpocket called a cutpurse.*

SOURCE E

▲ *Two kinds of beggars. On the left a soap eater, who made his mouth froth to look like an epileptic. On the right a Tom O'Bedlam who pretended to be mad.*

INVESTIGATION

You are the investigator!

Write a guide on 'How to Stay Alive in London'. You will need to mention:

- The different kinds of beggars.
- Secret language of criminals.
- Dangers to be avoided.
- Ways to defend yourself.

A life at a glance

YOUR MISSION: to investigate the life of Sir Henry Unton, Elizabethan gentleman.

THE EVENTS IN THE LIFE OF SIR HENRY

Look at the picture. On it somewhere are pictures to illustrate all the events listed below. The order of this list has been muddled up. But in the picture they tell the story of his life.

- Dying in France, 1596;
- Student at Oxford;
- Memorial in Faringdon church;
- His birth;
- Body brought home;
- Travelling in Italy;
- Funeral service at Faringdon church, Oxfordshire;
- Soldier in Holland and Belgium;
- At a banquet at his home at Wadley, Berkshire;
- Funeral procession.

INVESTIGATION

You are the investigator!

Use the picture and list of events to tell the life of Sir Henry Unton:

1. Identify which parts of the picture illustrate each of the events in Sir Henry's life. Are any events hard to put in the right order?

2. Plan out what happened in his life in the order in which the events occurred.

3. Now tell the story of Sir Henry's life, death and burial.

THIS CHAPTER ASKS

Why were women controlled by men?
How was marriage organised?
How much power did women have?

MEN AND WOMEN

Women lived much of their lives under the control of men – firstly their father, then (for most) a husband. It was thought:

■ God had made men to rule women;
■ Men were more intelligent than women;
■ Women were weak and more likely to sin than men were;
■ Women were gossips;
■ Women were not capable of coping with the responsibilities that men carried.

A girl could be married once she was aged 12, a boy at 14. However, most girls were about 15 when they married and most boys were aged about 20. Many rich marriages were arranged by parents, though the bride and groom were supposed to agree. However some were forced into marriages. Amongst poorer people there was greater freedom to choose the person that they wanted to marry.

Divorce was virtually impossible and Henry VIII (with his six wives) was not typical of ordinary people.

BABY AFTER BABY AFTER...

Women in the 16th, 17th and 18th centuries were often pregnant. A women might give birth a dozen times between the ages of fifteen and forty. This was because there were no **contraceptives**. As well as being hard work childbirth was dangerous.

In an age before **microscopes** and knowledge of germs, many women died from infections. Jane Seymour – Henry VIII's third wife – died soon after giving birth to the future King Edward VI. Many babies died too. Queen Anne (queen between 1702 and 1714) was pregnant eighteen times, but all her babies died.

Many rich women employed a wet nurse to care for their babies. These women fed the babies with milk from their own breasts. But this was always a worry as it was thought that a baby took its character from the milk it drank. So if the wet nurse drank too much it was feared the baby would grow up to be an alcoholic. If there was any blood in the milk, it was thought the baby would become a murderer!

SOURCE A

▲ *Elizabeth Vernon, a lady at court. She caused a scandal in 1598 by becoming pregnant while unmarried. Unmarried mothers were treated much worse than the fathers.*

WOMEN AND POWER

Most positions of power were held by men. Women were usually not well educated. Although some served as **churchwardens**, officials on country manors or school teachers, few became really powerful. But their rights did increase slightly. Some women owned shops and carried on a trade. In London married women were allowed to trade separately from their husbands. Even within marriage, women had power over the household and the servants.

In the 1580s a Dutch visitor to England, Emanuel Van Meteren, was surprised at the freedom married women had to play cards, chat with their friends, choose their own clothes, and go to social gatherings with other women.

> On a wedding night all the guests crowded into the bedroom to watch the newly wed couple go to bed together for the first time.

One way a women could increase her power was by marrying. If she married a wealthy man and he died, she could find herself in charge of great wealth. Elizabeth Talbot married four times as each husband died, and each time she inherited their wealth. She ended up as Countess of Shrewsbury, the richest woman in England after the queen and the builder of Hardwick Hall in Derbyshire – a house a queen would have been proud of. But not many women did as well as 'Bess of Hardwick'; most continued to live under the control of a man.

SOURCE B

▲ *A picture of the Cholmondeley sisters, painted in 1600. They were twins who were married on the same day and had their first baby on the same day!*

Q

1 a. Construct a spider diagram to show ways in which women were treated, or thought of, as inferior to men.

b. Colour code this with different colours to show *religious*, *social* and *economic* ways they were regarded as inferior.

2. How did childbirth make it difficult for women to challenge the power of men?

3. How powerless were women? Mention:
- Things that reduced their power.
- Ways women could get power.
- Your overall conclusion.

Women in charge?

EXCEPTIONS TO THE RULE

In almost all areas of life women were controlled by men. However, there was one exception to this strict rule. This was when a woman was a queen. Then, of course, she had power over men and they had to obey her. Between 1500 and 1750 there were four women who ruled as queens. They were: Mary (1553–8), Elizabeth (1558–1603), Mary II (1689–94) and Anne (1702–14).

SHOULD QUEENS RULE?

It was fine if a king married a woman and she became queen because then the man would be in charge. But what if a queen didn't marry? Many people in the 16th century were unhappy about women rulers. Henry VIII was desperate to have a son because he thought a woman could not cope. When one woman first met Queen Elizabeth I she said, in shock, 'Oh! Lord! – the Queen is a woman! How can this be!' But were even queens fully in control of men?

NEW WORDS

KEEP: take care of.
ROLES: ways you are expected to behave.
SUBJECTION: being controlled by.
WANTON: living badly, uncontrolled.

Queen Anne was always short but, after a lifetime giving birth, she was so short and fat when she died that her coffin was almost square.

SOURCE A

You have set to rule over us a woman, who was made by nature to be in **subjection** to a man. Ah, Lord, to take away the kingdom from a man and give it to a woman, seems to show how angry you are towards Englishmen.

◀ *A prayer, written by Thomas Becon in 1553, when Henry VIII's daughter, Mary, was crowned queen of England.*

SOURCE B

Nature made women to **keep** the home and nourish their family and children and not to meddle with important matters, nor to hold office in a city or council any more than children and babies do.

▲ *Written in 1565 by Sir Thomas Smith, a member of the government of Queen Elizabeth I.*

SOURCE C

Women are of two sorts: some of them are wiser, better educated and more trustworthy than a number of men; but some are foolish, **wanton**, witless, feeble, proud, gossips and in everyway the dregs of the devil's dunghill.

▲ *From a sermon preached to Queen Elizabeth I, by Bishop Aylmer, in 1583.*

Q
1. List the negative attitudes towards women in the sources.
2. Why do you think the writer of **Source C** said there were two kinds of woman? Think about who was listening.
3. How useful are these sources to an historian trying to decide how good women were as rulers of the country?

▲ **Queen Mary** (1553–8) was intelligent and tough, but when she married King Philip of Spain she had to share power with him and was desperate for a baby.

▲ **Queen Elizabeth I** (1558–1603) This shows her as a young queen. She never married and even paintings of her when she was an old woman had to show her as young and beautiful. All the men at court had to pretend they were in love with her.

Queen Mary II ➤ (1689–94) was daughter of the previous king, James II, but thought it wrong to have power over her husband William, so ruled with him. He made most of the decisions, and on coins it was his head that was first.

Q 'Even queens could not avoid the **roles** that women were expected to play'. Explain how this was true using examples from the four queens on this page. Think about:

■ Romance.
■ Pregnancies.
■ Husbands controlling wives.

▲ **Queen Anne** (1702–14) relied greatly on her husband's advice, though he was never made king. She was pregnant eighteen times and it ruined her health.

What you see, is what you get?

YOUR MISSION: to investigate how Elizabeth I used royal portraits as propaganda.

SOURCE **A**

NON SINE SOLE
IRIS.

NEW WORDS

ARMADA: great fleet of ships sent by Philip of Spain, in 1588, to carry an army to invade England.
ERMINE: a stoat in its white winter fur, which was used on royal robes.
PROPAGANDA: information used to carry a particular message or ideas.

◄ *The 'Rainbow Portrait' painted in 1600, probably by Isaac Oliver. At this date Elizabeth was 67 years old.*

A portrait is a painting showing what a person looks like. But is it? A painter can be told to make a person look a certain way. A painter can decide to put things in a picture that were not really there. A painting is not a photograph – it is a point of view, an interpretation of what a person is like. During Queen Elizabeth I's reign she used portraits of herself to send messages to her people. Others did the same thing about her. The pictures told of a good, wonderful, wise, beautiful and powerful ruler. They were full of clues, hints and messages. Can you read the clues? Can you understand the messages?

SOURCE B

◄ *The 'Ermine* Portrait' *painted in 1585 by Nicholas Hilliard.*

INVESTIGATION

You are the investigator!
On portraits of Elizabeth certain clues were used to carry messages:

- Swords show justice and power.
- A crown means she is truly Queen.
- Ermine shows a pure queen.
- A snake stands for wisdom.
- Long hair, or low-cut dress, shows a virgin.
- Flowers stand for youth.
- A rainbow, or olive branch, stands for peace.
- Decorative eyes or ears mean the ruler has great knowledge.
- A hand on a globe means power.
- Black and white were the colours of the legendary 'Queen of Corinth', who was pure and wise.

Use the clues, break the 'code'. Decide what each portrait is trying to tell you about Queen Elizabeth I.

SOURCE C

◄ *The 'Armada* Portrait' *painted about 1588 by George Gower. The ships on the left are the Spanish Armada, those on the right are the same ships showing the storms that wrecked them.*

33

THIS CHAPTER ASKS

Who were the enemies of England?
Why did Philip of Spain try to invade England?
How great a threat was Mary Queen of Scots?
Why did the Armada fail?

NEW WORDS

EXCOMMUNICATE: to cut off from the Church and from God. Catholics believed the Pope had the power to do this.

EMPIRE: a group of countries, peoples and lands under the control of one country.

Elizabeth's greatest European rivals, in the 1570s and 1580s, were Philip II of Spain and Henry III of France. Conflicts with the French had been going on since the Norman Conquest. The French king supported the claim of Mary, Queen of Scotland, to the throne of England. Spain had got on well with England, but this changed after 1560. The Spanish helped Catholic priests sent to England by the pope to try to make England Catholic again. English seaman clashed with the Spanish over the right to trade with the 'New World' of America. The old friendship died.

HUSBANDS OR ENEMIES?

The French and Spanish were rivals for power in Europe. To start with each hoped they might persuade Elizabeth to join with them to fight the other. Both Philip II and Henry III tried to persuade Elizabeth to marry them. Elizabeth managed to keep them both hopeful, without marrying either of them, or anyone else. After ten years of trying to get Elizabeth to join them, both France and Spain turned against England. But Spain was the biggest danger since France was weakened by religious civil wars. In fact, after 1589, when Protestant Henry of Navarre became king of France, relations between England and France improved, but England and Spain remained at war until 1604.

TROUBLE WITH THE POPE

The Catholic pope had hoped, at first, that Elizabeth might return to the Catholic Church. She was careful to keep him hoping without actually doing it. In the end he, too, lost patience. In 1568 Elizabeth imprisoned her cousin, Mary Queen of Scots, a Catholic driven out of Scotland by Protestant rebels. Elizabeth feared that English Catholics might try to replace her with Mary. On top of this, Mary was the widow of a French king, Francis. The French continued to support her. She was just too dangerous to let go free. Or so Elizabeth thought. The angry pope **excommunicated** Elizabeth and encouraged English Catholics to overthrow her. In 1569 Elizabeth defeated a revolt in northern England which was in support of Mary.

English people got on so badly with foreigners in the 16th century, that it was said at the time that it was easier to find a flock of white crows than an English person who liked foreigners.

SOURCE A

▲ Spanish soldiers kill Dutch Protestants, 1567. Elizabeth later helped the Dutch.

ELIZABETH FLEXES HER MUSCLES!

In the 1570s and 1580s Elizabeth had few friends in Europe. At this time she turned to supporting smaller Protestant nations – like the Dutch – who were fighting to free themselves from Spanish control. At this time Spain ruled the Netherlands as part of its great **Empire**.

English money, weapons and supplies were sent to help the Dutch. In 1585 an English army was sent to help them against Spain. In 1587 Elizabeth had Mary executed. This was all too much for Philip of Spain and, with the support of the pope, he prepared to invade England. The failure of this plan, when the Spanish Armada was defeated in 1588, meant Elizabeth no longer had to fear the power of Spain.

I'll do what I can to keep them from attacking; but Spain is the bigger danger as France has so many problems.
Elizabeth I

We are old enemies of England; Elizabeth won't help me fight Spain; she's executed my relative, Mary.
Henry III

Elizabeth is a Protestant heretic; she should be overthrown and replaced with a Catholic ruler.
The Pope

We were once friends with England but Elizabeth refuses to marry me; the English attack my ships, Protestant Elizabeth has murdered Catholic Mary Queen of Scots.
Philip II

Q

1. Imagine you are giving advice to Elizabeth shortly after she became queen in 1558. Would you advise her to:

■ Marry the ruler of France
■ Marry the ruler of Spain
■ Marry no one?

Along with your advice, explain why you think this is the best course of action.

2. France was an old enemy of England. Spain was an old friend. Why, by the end of the 16th century, had this changed?

3. From the information in the text and on the map, imagine that you are, in turn, Philip II, Henry III and the pope. Explain what you feel about Elizabeth and why you feel as you do. Think about:

■ The history of your relationship with England.
■ Religious beliefs.
■ The actions of the English.
■ Your own problems.

The death of Mary Queen of Scots

YOUR MISSION: to decide if Elizabeth was right to execute Mary Queen of Scots.

'ROMANTIC FICTION' OR 'HORROR STORY'?

The life of Mary Queen of Scots reads like a novel. Mary Stuart was the daughter of the king of Scotland, great grand-daughter of Henry VII, and relative of Queen Elizabeth I. Mary had problems with men. She married the heir to the throne of France and became Queen of France *and* Scotland when he became King Francis II. But he died young and she returned to Scotland. There she married an English nobleman, Lord Darnley. The marriage was very unhappy. In 1566 the jealous Darnley and his friends dragged Mary's Italian servant, David Riccio, away from Mary and stabbed him to death. Then, in 1567, Darnley's house was blown up and he was found strangled in the garden. Everyone blamed a Scottish nobleman, James Bothwell, but Mary married Bothwell! Her horrified enemies arrested her. She escaped. They defeated her. Mary escaped to England in 1568. Elizabeth I had her locked up and, nineteen years later, executed her. Are you following the plot? The question is – why did Elizabeth kill Mary Stuart? Was it right? Was it wise? Why did she do it?

When the executioner picked up Mary's head, her famous red hair came off – it was a wig. And out from under her skirts crept her little dog. Afterwards, it refused to eat and starved to death.

Mary Stuart

I should be queen after Elizabeth but I did not plan to kill her. In secret letters I just asked foreign friends for 'help' – I only meant them to free me. When a man called Babington offered to free me, I agreed. I was desperate to be free.

I'm Elizabeth's chief spy. Mary is dangerous. As long as she's alive, Catholics will rebel. In 1569 northern lords rebelled to make Mary heir to the throne. In 1584 there was a French plot to free Mary. And Mary's guilty of treason herself. In 1571 Mary was involved in a plot to bring Spanish soldiers to free her, and in 1586 she agreed to a plan by Anthony Babington to free her and kill Elizabeth.

Sir Francis Walsingham

I'm another of Elizabeth's ministers. In 1580 the pope said it was fine to kill Elizabeth. In 1584 Catholic terrorists murdered the Dutch Protestant ruler. Elizabeth is in real danger. In 1586 Mary made the king of Spain her heir instead of her own son. Now he'll be keen to get rid of Elizabeth.

Lord Burghley

I'm the queen's secretary. We told her Spanish troops had landed in Wales (which they hadn't) – and so she signed Mary's death warrant in 1587, but did not want it sent! I sent it anyway, to get rid of Mary. Now Elizabeth's blaming me.

William Davison

It's wrong to execute a queen – I won't do it. And if I did it would only annoy Spain and France who are Mary's friends. Also, it may annoy James VI, the young king of Scotland, as Mary is his mother.

Elizabeth

Elizabeth has said I'll rule England when she dies. I'll not fall out with England over my mother's execution. Especially as Elizabeth has told me she did not order the killing.

James VI

INVESTIGATION

You are the investigator!

Elizabeth is having second thoughts about the killing of Mary. She has asked you to investigate and see if you think she did the right thing or not. Write a report for the queen.

■ Was Mary guilty of plotting against Elizabeth?

■ Was Mary a danger to Elizabeth?

■ What problems might come from executing Mary?

Should Elizabeth have killed her? Was it just? Was it wise?

The defeat of the Spanish Armada

YOUR MISSION: to discover why the Spanish Armada failed.

In 1588 King Philip II of Spain sent a great fleet commanded by the Duke of Medina Sidonia to invade England. Philip was angry because:

- Elizabeth refused to marry him;
- English sailors had attacked Spanish ships carrying treasure back to Spain from America (see page 52);
- the English had helped the Dutch rebel against their Spanish rulers;
- Elizabeth had executed Mary Queen of Scots.

KING PHILIP'S PLAN

The plan was to sail up the English channel and pick up a Spanish army, commanded by the Duke of Parma, at the port of Calais in France. The Armada would then carry this army to England, to defeat Elizabeth and make England a Catholic country, friendly to Spain. The plan failed. Of the 150 Spanish ships that set out, only 67 returned to Spain.

Map made in 1588 to show the route of the Armada. The English attacked it as it sailed along the Channel but did not sink a single Spanish ship. At Calais the English sent fire ships into the anchored Spanish fleet causing a panic. Then a strong wind made it impossible for the Spanish to sail back down the channel. Instead they sailed round the north of Scotland where storms wrecked most of them. ▼

NEW WORDS

MILDER: calmer and less stormy.

FIRE SHIPS: old ships, set on fire, and sent into an enemy fleet to burn it.

SOURCE B

The sailing of the Armada should be delayed to allow the weather to grow **milder**. A king with your reputation should not be swept away by a thirst for revenge.

▲ *Written by the Spanish noble, Marquis de Santa Cruz, to Philip in 1587. Philip ignored his advice.*

SOURCE A

SOURCE C

The English with their excellent ships did not fight as expected but kept at a distance and fired at the hulls and sails of their enemy. The English set eight ships on fire amongst the Spanish fleet. Their enemy were woken up and had to cut their cables to get away from their anchors.

▲ *Written by Petruccio Ubaldini in 1588.*

SOURCE D

Even if the Armada supplies us with 6,000 Spaniards as promised, I shall still have too few troops. In a very short time my army will be so reduced as to be unable to cope with the great number of the enemy.

▲ *The Duke of Parma writes to Philip, 1588. Because Parma was not ready, the Armada was delayed off Calais, waiting for him.*

SOURCE E

They were in disorder, we followed them and there was a cruel fight. They lost a dozen of their best ships, some sunk and the rest run ashore. After God gave us victory they made haste to get away. We followed them but we turned back when we found in the whole fleet we did not have enough ammunition to fight.

▲ *Written by Sir Robert Carey, who was in one of the English ships. He is describing what happened after the English sent fireships amongst the Spanish anchored off Calais and forced the Spanish north out of the English Channel.*

SOURCE F

▲ *Treasure from the Armada ship, Gerona. Like most of the Spanish ships that were lost, it was destroyed by storms off the coast of Ireland.*

INVESTIGATION

You are the investigator!
Imagine Philip II has given you the job of explaining why his Armada has failed. Write him a report using the evidence.

■ Remind him what the plan was for the Armada.

■ Use the evidence to suggest different reasons why it failed.

■ Explain what eventually happened to the Armada.

■ Conclude with saying what you think was the single biggest cause of its failure and why.

THE BIG PICTURE

THIS CHAPTER ASKS
What happened during the rule of the Stuarts?
Why was there a plot to kill King James I?

The Stuarts are the family who ruled Britain between 1603 and 1714. During this time there was a Civil War, Plague, the Fire of London, two kings were overthrown (one of these was killed), and another nearly murdered. And all in about one hundred years. It sounds more like a soap opera than history. This is the story of the Stuarts. An everyday family of royals ...

NEW WORDS

DIVINE RIGHT: ruler because God made it so. He thought he did not have to answer to Parliament.
REPUBLIC: ruled without a king, or queen.
TOAST: to drink and make a happy wish for someone.

1603–5

'Good Queen Bess' died childless. James VI of Scotland, becomes King James I of England. Believed in Divine Right. In 1605, Guy Fawkes nearly blew him up.

1611

King James version of the Bible translated into English.

1625

James died. New king – Charles I – believed he could rule without Parliament. No Parliament 1629–40.

1630s–1640s

Puritans wanted simpler services, thought Church of England too Catholic. Charles against Puritans.

1640–49

Scots rebelled. Charles short of money. Called parliament. Charles fell out with parliament. Civil War in 1642. Charles lost. 1649 executed. Britain a republic.

Q

1. Look at the following dates. Explain why they were important in the story of the Stuart family: 1603, 1642, 1660, 1688, 1714.

2. Choose two dates that you think were important in the changing history of how the countries in Britain were run. Say why they were important.

William III died when his horse tripped in a molehill. Jacobites drank **toasts** to the 'little gentleman in black velvet' (the mole)!

1653
Oliver Cromwell ruled Britain as Lord Protector.

1660–6
Charles's son, Charles II, returned as king in 1660.

Great Plague,1665, then Fire of London, 1666.

1685–8
Charles II died. New king – his Catholic brother, James II – was unpopular. James overthrown in 1688. Replaced by his daughter Mary and her Dutch husband William III. The 'Glorious Revolution'.

1690
William defeated Irish Catholics.

1688–1708
In France, James and his son, also James, and friends (the Jacobites) plotted to return.

First Jacobite revolts, 1689, 1708. Both failed.

1702
William died. Replaced by Mary's sister, Anne.

1707
Scotland and England united. One parliament, in London, for both.

1714
HERE LIES THE BODY OF QUEEN ANNE 1665-1714 R.I.P

Anne died without children. New king, George I, from Hanover, in Germany.

Was Guy Fawkes 'set up'?

YOUR MISSION: to discover if the Gunpowder Plotters were 'set up'.

One hour before midnight on 4 November 1605, the soldiers of King James I searched the cellars under the Houses of Parliament. They were looking for Catholic traitors trying to blow up the king. James knew all about the dangers of **gunpowder** – his father's house had been blown up in 1567 and his father murdered. James feared **assassins** and wore a padded jacket in case anyone tried to stab him!

In the cellars the soldiers found a man beside 36 kegs of gunpowder. He was Guy Fawkes and two days later – after being tortured – he confessed that he and other Catholics had been plotting to blow up Protestant King James.

A RATHER STRANGE LETTER

One of the plotters named by Fawkes was called Francis Tresham. He was the cousin of the Catholic Lord Monteagle. This is interesting because, nine days before Guy Fawkes was discovered, Lord Monteagle had received an **anonymous** letter. In it he was warned to stay away from Parliament when the king was going to be there on 5 November. Monteagle was loyal to James and so he took the warning to the king.

GETTING RID OF THE WITNESSES?

After Fawkes was captured, the king's soldiers traced the rest of the plotters to Holbeche House, in Staffordshire. There all the leaders of the revolt were killed. Tresham died mysteriously in prison. None of those who knew how the plot had been planned lived to tell their story.

NEW WORDS

ANONYMOUS: when it is not known who wrote something.
ASSASSIN: a killer.
GUNPOWDER: a powder that will explode when fire touches it.
RETIRE: leave and go somewhere else.
TOLERANT: allowing people to live the way they please.

SOURCE A

Retire into the country where you can expect the event in safety, for though there is no appearance of danger, yet I tell you they shall receive a terrible blow this Parliament but they shall not see who hurts them.

▲ *Part of the anonymous letter sent to Monteagle.*

SOURCE B

It was demanded if he were not sorry for so foul a treason and he answered that he was sorry for nothing but that he had not succeeded. The king asked him how he could conspire so hideous a treason? He answered that a dangerous 'disease' required a desperate remedy [cure].

◄ *A account of the questioning of Guy Fawkes, written by an eye witness, Sir Edward Holby, on 19 November 1605.*

SOURCE C

It is certain that Lord Salisbury [One of James's ministers] already knew of the plot before Fawkes's arrest, because all the plotters were being watched. He let the plot continue in order to make the arrest a dramatic one.

◄ *Tudors and Stuarts, David Kennedy, 1981.*

THE EFFECTS ON CATHOLICS

Before the plot, James had been **tolerant** to Catholics. For example, they no longer had to pay fines for refusing to attend Protestant Church services. This worried some members of his government who feared that if they were not treated harshly the numbers of Catholics might increase.

After the Gunpowder Plot, Parliament passed strict laws against Catholics.

SOURCE **D**

▲ *The plot was used by the government to stir up anti-Catholic feeling. This picture was drawn, giving the government view. It shows the devil, the pope, the king of Spain and Catholic priests in a tent, planning the plot and a devil leading Fawkes to the gunpowder. But God has seen what is happening and will stop the plot.*

WHAT WAS GOING ON?

The simple answer is that historians are not sure. There are a number of different interpretations:

- It was a genuine plot and the king was lucky to discover it because Tresham warned his cousin!
- It was a genuine plot but some government spies knew all about it. They warned Monteagle but let the plot go on to let Catholics get blamed.
- The whole thing was set up by the government and Fawkes and the rest were innocent victims.

Did you know?

- No one ever found the 'tunnel' that Fawkes confessed the plotters had tried to dig before they managed to hire a cellar under Parliament.
- No Catholic would have been allowed to buy gunpowder. Only the government could sell it.
- The man who rented the cellars to the plotters died suddenly on 5 November.
- Strangely, no one saw 36 kegs of gunpowder being taken in.
- The plotters were allowed to rent a cellar under Parliament despite being known Catholics.

INVESTIGATION

You are the investigator!

Explain anything odd about the way in which the plot was carried out, or the plotters were treated.

Look at the possible interpretations on this page. Decide which you think best fits the evidence and explain why you think this.

8 A WAR WITHOUT AN ENEMY

THIS CHAPTER ASKS

Why was there civil war in England?
How was the war fought?
What was the impact on the country?

THE ENGLISH CIVIL WAR

Between 1642 and 1646 King Charles I fought a civil war against his enemies in Parliament. It was a war which he had lost by 1646. In January 1649 the king was executed by beheading. In 1643 the royalist and parliamentary armies fought at Landsdown, near Bath. Before the battle the royalist commander, Sir Ralph Hopton, wrote to his friend, Sir William Waller, commander of the army of Parliament.

It was a sad letter in which Hopton wrote, 'I detest this war without an enemy'. At the end of the day Hopton lay dead and, by the end of the war, perhaps a quarter of the nation's adults had taken part in fighting that had torn the country apart. So, eventually, many people had discovered plenty of enemies to fight. Why did this war happen? As with lots of questions in history, the answer is not simple. It depends who you ask.

Q

1. Why do you think Sir Ralph Hopton called the Civil War a 'war without an enemy'?

2. Look at the possible causes of the Civil War. Which ones are *political*, which *religious*, which *economic*?

3. Historians do not agree about what caused the Civil War. Using the evidence on this BIG PICTURE explain why this is so.

> The war was caused by the king ruling without Parliament for eleven years. He took money, called 'Ship Money', instead of taxes that we agreed to. Any enemies he punished in his Court of Star Chamber. We're fighting to protect the power of Parliament, the people and the laws of England

Puritan member of the House of Commons

> The war was caused by the House of Commons trying to take away the power of the king. Most of us lords support the king. He can rule without Parliament if he wishes. We're fighting to protect the power of the king, the people and the laws of England.

Member of the House of Lords

THE BIG PICTURE

THE YEARS OF THE SWORD

We usually talk about *the* English Civil War but really there were a number of wars. The first and greatest lasted from 1642 until 1646, and the king lost it. The Second Civil War was fought in 1648; this time against Royalists and Scots who had fallen out with Parliament. Between 1649 and 1650 the parliamentary leader, Cromwell, defeated Catholic Ireland.

Next, between 1650 and 1651, Cromwell beat the Scots again and then beat Charles II (royalist leader after the execution of his father, in 1649) at the battle of Worcester. Fighting finally stopped in 1652.

At the end of these wars Parliament had won and the most powerful parliamentary general was Oliver Cromwell. He ruled Britain until he died in 1658. With no strong ruler to replace him, Parliament asked Charles II to return in 1660.

1642
Charles set up his capital at Oxford. Charles tried to capture London. Stopped at Battle of Turnham Green.

1643
Battle of Newbury. Royalists stopped from marching on London.

1644
Scots joined side of Parliament.

1644
Royalists defeated at Battle of Marston Moor.

1644–5
Parliament formed New Model Army. Better run and paid, to beat Charles.

New Model Army beat Charles at Battle of Naseby.

1646–9 *King surrendered to the Scots, who sold him to Parliament. Second Civil War. Royalists defeated.*

1649 Charles executed.

1649–50 *Cromwell beat royalists and Catholics in Ireland.*

1650 *Scots fell out with Parliament. Cromwell beat Scots at Battle of Dunbar.*

1651 *Cromwell beat Charles II at Battle of Worcester.*

1653–7 *Cromwell fell out with Parliament. He became Lord Protector. Cromwell refused Army's idea that he become king, though he ruled like a king.*

1658–60 *Cromwell died. Charles II returned as king; the Restoration.*

In 1660 Cromwell's body was dug up and his head chopped off and stuck on a pole. Later it was put on display at various times and, in 1960, it was buried at a secret spot in a Cambridge University chapel.

Q 1. Why is it really a mistake to talk about *the English Civil War*? Think about:

■ the number of wars;
■ countries involved.

Discussion Point
Would you have supported Charles I or Parliament? Explain why.

Cromwell – hero or villain?

MILITARY GENIUS OR BRUTAL KILLER?

Oliver Cromwell is one of the most famous people in British history. He was a farmer from East Anglia who became an MP, and then went on to become the most successful Parliamentary general in the Civil War.

Cromwell's skill as a soldier led to the defeat of the Royalist forces at the Battle of Naseby (1645) and broke the power of the king. He crushed the Scots at the Battle of Dunbar (1650), and at the Battle of Worcester (1651) he destroyed Charles II's hopes of making himself king. In these battles Cromwell showed himself to be both brave and merciful to his enemies.

In Ireland, Cromwell put down a rebellion that had been going on since 1641, destroying his Royalist and Catholic enemies with great brutality and ruthlessness. Thousands died and in Ireland Cromwell is remembered as a killer of innocent men, women and children.

NEW WORDS

COURTS MARTIAL: courts run by the army.

RUMP: the back end, all that is left of something.

UNELECTED: not voted for in elections.

The Parliament Cromwell set up in 1653 to replace the Rump was called Barebone's Parliament after one of its Puritan members, Praise-God Barebone.

SOURCE A

At first how glorious, he destroyed all the enemies of Parliament but then such betrayal. His ambition overtook him and he crushed us underfoot and all that would oppose him he had removed.

▲ *Written in 1698 by Edmund Ludlow. Ludlow had fought alongside Cromwell but disagreed with him taking control of the country in 1654.*

SOURCE B

I would rather live seven years under the old king's government at its worse than under this government. We were ruled before by king, lords and Commons. Now we are ruled by a general, **courts martial** and the Commons. What's the difference?

▲ *John Lilburne in 1649. Lilburne was a Leveller leader who thought Cromwell had betrayed the people by not giving ordinary people the vote.*

SOURCE C

Death has finally turned the tables on him [Cromwell] and confined all his ambition, all his cruel plans into the narrow width of a grave.

▲ *Lucy Hutchinson, after Cromwell's death in 1658. Lucy disliked Cromwell after he fell out with her husband.*

SOURCE D

People look back on the days of Oliver Cromwell and praise him so. What brave things he did and, oh, how the neighbouring princes did fear him.

▲ *Written by Samuel Pepys in 1667. Pepys was a member of the government under King Charles II.*

SOURCE E

The days of Oliver Cromwell were marvellous days of prosperity, freedom, peace.

▲ *Written by a Bristol Baptist in 1685. Puritan religious believers like this had greater freedom under Cromwell.*

SOURCE F

Clever Crumwells Cabinet Councell Discoverd

▲ *A Royalist picture showing Cromwell and the Parliamentary leaders getting orders from the devil.*

SOURCE G

Cromwell, our chief of men, guided by faith and matchless fortitude, to peace and truth
Thy glorious way hast ploughed.

▲ *Written by the poet John Milton, a friend of Cromwell.*

SOURCE H

We can see him as the firey fighter for freedom, or the clever politician using all his skills to keep a hated army rule going.

▲ *Written by the historian Christopher Hill in God's Englishman, 1970.*

REVOLUTIONARY OR BETRAYER OF THE PEOPLE?

It was Cromwell who argued that King Charles I should be executed in 1649. After the death of the king, Cromwell opposed those in the army, called the Levellers, who wanted to give the vote to ordinary men and reward them for opposing the king. Cromwell and the army leaders made it clear that while they had been prepared to kill the king they did not want to give power to the poor. They feared this would lead to chaos and the rich losing control.

In 1653 Cromwell lost patience with Parliament because it would not do as he wished. This Parliament was called the **Rump** because it was all that was left after those who opposed Cromwell and the army leadership had been thrown out. Now Cromwell even threw out the Rump MPs. After this, Cromwell experimented with different kinds of governments – firstly with parliaments made up of **unelected** Puritans he thought he could work with, later with major generals from the army running parts of England. None of these really worked properly. Cromwell – who took the title Lord Protector – even considered an idea to make him king, but rejected it.

People at the time and since are divided in their views of Cromwell. Was he a hero or a villain? What do you think?

Q **1.** Read each source and the information about it. Explain what picture of Cromwell each gives and how reliable it is.

2. Read **Source H**. What different pieces of evidence might Christopher Hill have used to support these two different views of Cromwell?

3. From all you have read, explain how the evidence can be used to make Cromwell seem both a *hero* and a *villain*.

How did the war affect people's lives?

YOUR MISSION: to decide in what ways the Civil War affected the lives of ordinary people.

INVESTIGATION

NEW WORDS

DESOLATION: ruined and destroyed.

PLUNDERED: robbed.

There is a famous story, which tells how, in July 1644, the Royalist and Parliamentary armies were facing each other near York. They were about to fight the battle of Marston Moor. Suddenly, someone noticed a farmer was busily ploughing his field between the two armies. A soldier went to tell him that he was in the way and would he mind moving so they could get on with the battle! He didn't know what the fuss was all about until it was explained to him that the king and Parliament were in the middle of a Civil War. Astonished, he asked, 'Why, has they two fallen out again?' Then he packed up his plough and hurried off. The battle started.

Think again. It's a nice story but could anyone have really not noticed that the country was in the middle of a civil war? Is it really possible? Look at the evidence and decide.

SOURCE A

I have lent money to both sides. Been **plundered** by both sides. Been imprisoned by both sides. A mad world.

◀ *Written to the Earl of Middlesex, in 1643, from the person running his lands in Gloucestershire.*

SOURCE B

Give us the money you owe us within a week. If not, expect a frightening group of soldiers amongst you, from which if you hide yourself, they shall burn your houses without mercy, hang you if they find you and scare your ghosts.

▲ *Written to villagers at Evesham, from soldiers stationed nearby.*

SOURCE C

SOURCE D

The people of Carlisle were forced to eat rats and dogs and it is full of misery and **desolation**, as sword, famine and plague have left it.

▲ *A description of Carlisle by the soldiers who captured the town after a siege. Townspeople always suffered terribly in a siege.*

A cartoon drawn in the 1640s. It shows a soldier carrying things he has stolen. Look carefully and you can see a duck, roast chicken, cooking pot, sausages and cups. It is not clear which side he is on. ➤

SOURCE E

We are called to march, march, march, that a rich countryside is in front of us, but we find nothing by the way, all is deserted.

◄ *A message sent to London from the Scottish army marching through the Midlands of England in 1645.*

SOURCE F

Trade has stopped and decayed, especially the cotton cloth, butter, cheese and cattle from Wales and the malt and other goods traded into Wales. Our hay we used to get from Montgomeryshire – but that is now completely taken from us by the enemy.

▲ *A report from Shrewsbury Town Council to the local Royalist Commander, 1644.*

SOURCE G

I have had three horses taken from me, one after the other. Then my spade was taken to help build a fort, leaving me unable to grow my crops. I've got a family to support, the local taxes to pay and I have to feed and give shelter to a soldier.

▲ *Written in 1644 by a small farmer, living near Ludlow.*

SOURCE H

Soldiers from both sides steal from the estates of noblemen. Nobody seems to know what we have been fighting about all this time.

▲ *From a letter written by the Royalist Earl of Berkshire, in 1645.*

I NVESTIGATION

You are the investigator!

1. Look at the following groups of people, then use the sources of evidence to show how the war affected them:

■ townspeople and traders;

■ farmers and country-people;

■ rich landowners.

2. The historian Ronald Hutton had heard of the story of the ploughman at Marston Moor. He did not believe it was true and wrote: 'The Civil War was just not that sort of war.' Do you agree, or disagree with his opinion?

A picture drawn at the time, showing the Royalist Prince Rupert attacking and destroying the town of Birmingham in 1643. ▼

SOURCE I

9 BRITAIN AND THE WORLD

THIS CHAPTER ASKS

When did Britain begin its Empire?
Why did this start?
What was the attraction of settling in America?

NEW WORDS

COLONISTS: settlers in land abroad.
COLONY: land ruled by a country abroad.
CUSTOMS: taxes on goods paid at a port.

EXPLORERS OF A 'NEW WORLD'

On 24 June 1497, John Cabot, captain of the Bristol ship *Matthew,* became the first modern European to see the mainland of North America. Some years earlier, in 1492, Christopher Columbus had reached the islands of the Caribbean. Many centuries before this, Viking **colonists** had reached North America but their explorations had been lost in legends. Cabot was making modern history. At the time that Cabot sailed, the Collector of **Customs** in the Port of Bristol was named Richard ap Meryk, or Ameryk, and Bristolians still claim that the New World of America took its name from this Tudor Bristolian! Whatever the truth of this, it was in August that Cabot got back to Bristol with news of the huge numbers of codfish that could be caught off the *new founde lande* (eventually Newfoundland, off the Canadian coast).

RIVALS IN AMERICA

Between 1501 and 1506 the Bristol men sailed every year to America. In 1508 another Bristol ship explored the whole eastern coast of America, from Florida to Baffin Island in the north. But when they returned in 1509 they found that the new king – Henry VIII – was discouraging further exploration for fear of offending his allies, the Spanish, who were carving out an Empire for themselves in the new world. So, if Britain was beginning to take an interest in the world beyond Europe it was not going to be easy. Other European countries had plans to do so as well and were ready to fight to defend them.

In the 16th century, the great explorers were Spanish and Portugese. Both took lands in America and the Far East. But English sailors wanted a share and from 1570 began to raid Spanish trading posts in America and ships returning to Spain. One of the most famous was Francis Drake, who in 1577–80 sailed round the world, attacking Spanish ships. The growing bad feeling led to the Spanish Armada.

BUILDING AN EMPIRE?

By 1600 English merchants and explorers were sailing to America, Africa, Russia, India and the islands south-east of China called the East Indies. None of them were aiming to conquer land – they travelled to trade and bring goods home to Britain to sell. In 1603 the only land the English had captured abroad and managed to keep was in Ireland. Here both Elizabeth I and James I had driven the Catholic Irish from the best land and replaced them with Protestants from southern Scotland.

By 1750 this had changed. The British had gained an Empire in North America and the West Indies and were about to capture more land in India. No one had planned this. The first aims had been trade, particularly the trade in black slaves used in the farming of crops (sugar and tobacco) in America that were popular in Europe. But as Britain fought and won wars against the Dutch and Spanish in the 17th century, it captured land from them abroad. Then, after 1688, there were wars with France as the new Dutch ruler of England, William III, used the wealth of his new country to fight France, which was the old enemy of the Dutch.

THE BEGINNING OF THE EMPIRE IN INDIA

In India, the first English settlers had come only to trade but soon the collapse of the strong Indian Mughal Empire meant that Europeans could take and control land. The French and British were rivals in Europe and this soon spread to India in the 1740s.

The fighting on the British side was not organised by the government but by the traders of the East India Company, one of whose soldiers, Robert Clive, won great victories against the French. After the Battle of Plassey, in 1757, the East India Company found itself the ruler of large parts of India. Britain was becoming a world power, without planning to do so.

As a young man, Robert Clive twice tried to commit suicide but each time the pistol would not fire. He went on to defeat the French in India and later tried to commit suicide again. This time he succeeded.

Key Dates

1497 John Cabot sailed to America.

1583 Newfoundland **colony** failed.

1585 Virginia colony. It later failed.

1600 British East India Company begins trading with India.

1607 first successful English colony in Virgina, America.

1617 first tobacco plants grown in Virginia.

1643 sugar first grown in English colony of Barbados.

1649 Navigation Act. British take control of all trade with British colonies.

1655 British defeat Spain and take Jamaica.

1664 Britain captured New York from Dutch.

1704 Britain captured Gibraltar from Spanish.

1713 By this date British victories over the French had won Britain land in Canada.

1757 British East India Company defeat Indian and French army in India.

1759 British defeat French in Canada.

The development of the Britsh Empire, 1497–1760

N

Q 1. Look at the Key Dates. Some of them are important 'growth points' – events that made a big impact on the growth of a British Empire. Find three and explain why you chose these to be so important

2. Explain how the following helped an Empire to grow: *trade*, *wars*, *new crops*.

How wonderful was the New World?

INVESTIGATION

YOUR MISSION: to discover what the 'New World' of America was really like.

The first English colonies in America were failures. These were in Newfoundland in 1583 and on Roanoke Island, Virginia, between 1585 and 1590. At Roanoke the English adventurer, Sir Walter Raleigh, twice tried to set up a colony but each ended in disaster. Why? There were too few settlers, planning was poor, too few supplies, wars with Indians, lack of experience in crops that would grow in the 'New World'.

This changed on 13 May 1607, when a colony was set up at Jamestown, Virginia. It was from Jamestown that the real Captain John Smith was exploring when he met the Indian chief's daughter, Pocahontas. The organisers of the new colonies were desperate for people to come and join them. People wrote the most fantastic things about America in order to persuade people to risk their lives there – but what was it really like? Imagine you are planning to leave England to set up a new life in Virginia. But before you go, you want to find out what you are letting yourself in for!

NEW WORDS

FOWL: birds such as ducks and partridges.

HIGHWAYS: main roads.

VENISON: deer meat.

SOURCE A

The air is very clear and not at all foggy. We have grapes, strawberries, gooseberries and plums. Our corn is good but the peas were not worth gathering because the sun dried them. We have found the Indians very loving and we can walk as peaceably and safely in the woods as in the **highways** of England. We entertain them in our houses and they give us **venison**. I expect you and your friends will come and live in America.

▲ *Written in 1622 by Edward Winslow, who had lived in America for two years. His aim was to encourage other settlers to join him.*

SOURCE C

The summer is as hot as Spain, the winter cold as France or England. The heat of summer is in June, July and August, but usually the cold breezes reduce the great heat. The cold of winter is half December, January, February and half March. The cold is extremely sharp but here the proverb is true, that no extreme lasts a long time.

▲ *Written by the explorer Captain John Smith.*

SOURCE B

By investing £12, 10 shillings he shall be lord of 200 acres of land to him and his heirs forever. And if he pays for transporting himself, his family and tenants he shall be given for each person he pays for another 100 acres.

▲ *Information given out by the Virginia Company which organised settlement in America.*

SOURCE D

I will not tell you that corn grows naturally on trees, nor that the deer come when you call, or stand still while they are shot, nor that the fish leap into the cooking pot but there is **fowl**, deer and fish for the taking if men work hard.

▲ *Written in 1628 by Christopher Levett, who had lived in America for seven years.*

SOURCE E

◄ *A picture claiming to show what life was like in America in the 17th century. It shows hunting with hawks, dogs and guns, and fishing in the sea.*

A Welsh story claims that the real discoverer of America was the legendary Prince Madoc. The search for Welsh-speaking Indians went on into the 19th century. Not surprisingly, none were ever found!

SOURCE F

The Indians have no iron weapons, they have bows made of witch-hazell and arrows of reeds and wood about a yard long. In war we have the advantage in our discipline and in our weapons. In one battle about 700 were killed or taken prisoner.

▲ *Two settlers, Thomas Harriot and John Winthrop wrote about their experience of fighting Indians in Virginia.*

INVESTIGATION

You are the investigator!

So, what *is* life in 17th-century America really like?

1. a. Have a look at all the evidence and explain the different points of view.

b. Then decide which evidence you think sounds reliable, which unreliable, which you are not sure of.

c. After this, write what you think you have found out about:

■ The natural resources of America.
■ The weather and climate.
■ Relationships with the Indians.
■ Availability of land.

2. a. Now decide: will you go to settle in Virginia, or not?

b. Make your decision and explain the reasons for your choice.

Discussion Point

What problems are there in using films, like *Pocahontas*, to try to find out about history?

10 THE APPLIANCE OF SCIENCE

THIS CHAPTER ASKS
Why was there an increase in scientific discoveries in the 17th century?
How much did medicine improve?
Why did the great witchhunts end?
How did the plague affect life in London?

SCIENCE IN THE MODERN WORLD
Today we take science for granted. We assume that experiments take place to discover how things work. We carefully observe and record, and experiments are checked against other experiments. New technologies produce machines that allow us to understand more about the world. This way of thinking affects things as different as the way people treat illness, put space stations into orbit, change the genetic makeup of animals and crops, produce new forms of computer and information technology.

THE BEGINNING OF THE MODERN WORLD?
Some of these things improve our lives, some make them worse and, of course, there are vital questions about life that science cannot answer and will never answer. Nevertheless, it is clear that science affects our lives in a huge number of ways. This has not always been the case. Changes that led to this 'modern' way of understanding the world began in the 16th and 17th centuries. In 1662, the Royal Society was formed to encourage research. In 1676, the Royal Observatory was set up at Greenwich to study the stars.

Long-term causes of the 'Scientific Revolution'

Rediscovery of Greek and Roman ideas in the Renaissance led to questioning ideas common during the Middle Ages about health, the body, the universe.

Improved metalworking led to finer tools and instruments.

Better glassmaking led to improved magnifying lenses.

Challenging the Catholic Church led to questioning some religious ways of explaining events and problems.

Taking education away from the Church meant there was less control of it.

Invention of printing helped spread new ideas.

New, realistic art caused people to look more critically at how things were made.

Permission was granted for more dead bodies to be cut up.

HOW THE NEW IDEAS SHOWED THEMSELVES IN THE WORK OF KEY PEOPLE

▲ **William Harvey (1578–1657)** proved that the heart pumps blood round the body. Said problems in society not caused by witches.

▲ **Robert Boyle (1627–91)** established modern chemistry.

▲ **Isaac Newton (1642–1727)** worked on new ideas in maths, physics, astronomy. Discovered gravity and its effect on the Sun and planets.

▲ **Robert Hook (1635–1703)** worked on new ideas in maths and astronomy, and designed a microscope.

▲ **Christopher Wren (1632–1723)** worked on astronomy and architecture. Rebuilt St Paul's Cathedral in London in a classical (Roman and Ancient Greek) style.

William Harvey was a cool customer. In 1642 he was at the first Civil War Battle of Edgehill. He kept warm during the freezing night after the battle by pulling a dead body over himself, like a blanket.

Q

1. Look at the inventors. Which of the long-term causes of change might have led to each one's discoveries?

2. Which of these discoveries do you think was the most important and why?

3. Between 1450 and 1730 about 60,000 people across Europe were executed as witches. Between 1645 and 1647 Matthew Hopkins, called the Witchfinder General, was responsible for the deaths of 200 people in England accused of being 'witches'. What does that tell you about how 'scientific' the 17th century really was?

Discussion Point

In what ways does modern science make your life healthier?

How great was medical progress?

During the 17th century, important discoveries were made about the way the human body works and the way in which sick people should be treated. But a big question remains: how much did these discoveries really alter the way doctors and surgeons understood illness, or cured disease?

THE WORK OF WILLIAM HARVEY

In 1599 Harvey went to study at the great medical school at Padua in Italy. Before Harvey carried out his experiments, people had believed the Greek idea that dated back to the second century AD, that blood flowed out from the heart to all parts of the body, where it was burnt up like fuel. Harvey carried out scientific experiments which showed this idea was mistaken. Harvey found that, in reality, the heart pumped blood to the body through arteries, and the blood returned to the heart through veins. He proved this by:

- Cutting up live cold-blooded animals such as frogs. Their hearts beat slowly and could be watched working;
- Pushing thin wire down veins;
- Measuring the amount of blood the heart pumped;
- Trying to pump liquids past the valves in the veins. It could not be done, showing that blood only flowed one way.

The problem with Harvey's work was that, until the 19th-century discovery of germs and **anaesthetics**, surgery was so crude that few patients survived an operation. His discovery had little impact for two hundred years.

THE WORK OF RICHARD WISEMAN

Wiseman was surgeon to King Charles II. Wiseman realised that it was a mistake to just copy old ideas about medicine. He thought it was better to observe which treatments worked and which did not and to rely on practical experience. He was impressed by writers in other countries who were also experimenting with new treatments.

SOURCE A

I have read all the famous writers, yet in my writing I was more influenced by my own judgement and experience than other men's authority. I spent my time in armies, navies and cities, not in universities and books.

▲ Written by Richard Wiseman, surgeon to King Charles II. Wiseman says that practical experience is more important than copying ideas that are hundreds of years old.

NEW WORDS

ANAESTHETICS: putting patients to sleep during an operation.

BEZOAR STONE: a stone thought to be magical.

HUMOURS: the Ancient Greek idea that the body is made up of four elements: blood, yellow bile, black bile, phlegm. It was often treated by letting blood out of a sick person.

SOURCE B

I have heard him say that after his book on the Circulation of the Blood came out he lost a great many patients and 'twas believed he was crack-brained.'

▲ John Aubrey, a friend of Harvey, records the problems faced by Harvey.

SOURCE C

To cure malaria and the gout, take the hair and nails of the patient, cut them small, put them in a hole in an oak tree. Block up the hole with a peg made from the same tree.

▲ Written by W. Salmon in his Book of Remedies, 1682.

MORE TROUBLE FOR ANCIENT GREEK IDEAS

Other doctors rejected the Ancient Greek belief that illness was caused by an imbalance of **humours** in the body and could be cured by taking blood from a patient. This was very revolutionary at the time as it had been believed for many centuries that these Ancient Greek writers were correct and could not be rejected. One 17th-century doctor, who did reject them, helped a patient recover by ordering him a roast chicken and a bottle of wine instead of draining off blood like other doctors had done.

> Between 1660 and 1682 Charles II touched over 92,000 people with skin diseases.

SOURCE E

Removing 16 ounces (425 ml) of blood from the arm. Shaving the head and burning the skin. Sneezing powder. Putting hot tar on his feet and dried beetles on his head. Making him sick. Cutting his jugular vein and removing 10 ounces (300 ml) of blood. Forty drops of medicine made from human skull. Medicine containing **bezoar stone**.

⬆ *Treatments given to King Charles II by his doctors in the five days before he died in 1685.*

SOURCE F

For a bullet wound take out the bullet and pour in hot oil. On the second day it may be convenient for the body to be purged, thereby carrying off the sick humour.

⬆ *Written by Richard Wiseman. He knew the French surgeon, Paré, had shown that hot oil only made a wound worse but he still used it. Wiseman also carried on the Ancient Greek ideas of bleeding patients.*

SOURCE D

⬆ *Charles II touching people to 'cure' their skin diseases known as the 'King's Evil'. He and many of his doctors believed he could heal them because he was king.*

Q

1. Explain why Harvey and Wiseman were important in changing medical ideas. What problems did they face?

2. Look at **Sources C, D, E** and **F**. Explain how each one shows that changes in medicine were not really so great.

3. From what you have seen how great was progress in medicine?

■ Explain the importance of changes
■ Explain limits to changes and what stayed the same.

Why did the Great Witchhunt end?

In the 16th and 17th centuries most people believed in witches. They thought that problems in society were caused by people who worshipped the devil and used magic to cause harm to others. They believed that these witches surrounded themselves with evil spirits, or imps, disguised as animals. These imps did bad things for them. Most people accused of witchcraft were women but men were also accused at times. Between 1450 and 1730 about 100,000 people across Europe were accused of being witches and, of these, about 60,000 were killed. In reality, the vast majority of these were ordinary people being blamed for things they had not done.

HUNTING FOR WITCHES IN ENGLAND

Before 1450 very few people were accused of being witches but by 1542 laws were passed which meant a person found guilty of witchcraft could be executed. People became convinced that witches were the cause of the many problems facing the country. Any unpopular person could find themselves accused of witchcraft. King James VI and I was a keen witchhunter. He encouraged witchhunts in Scotland and later in England. In East Anglia, in the 1640s, Matthew Hopkins took the title 'Witchfinder General' and led an attack on people accused of witchcraft. In England witches were hanged; in Scotland they were burnt.

NEW WORDS

CONFESSIONS: admitting to a sin.

REPEALED: cancelled.

SOURCE B

His legs were crushed and beaten together. The bones and flesh were so bruised that the blood poured out.

▲ *A description of the torture of a Scottish 'witch' in 1591.*

SOURCE C

There were no witches, or other people thinking they were bewitched, until people talked and wrote about it.

▲ *The Spanish writer Alonso de Salazar wrote this in 1610.*

SOURCE A

▲ *A 17th-century picture showing a 'swimming test'.*

SOURCE D

The real turning point in the great hunt occurred when magistrates and judges came to the conclusion that the trials had led to the execution of innocent human beings and took steps to prevent such injustice from ever happening again.

▲ *Written by the historian, Brian Levack, in* The Witchhunt in Early Modern Europe, *1995.*

But how were witchfinders to prove a person was a witch? There were various tests. One, called the 'swimming test' involved putting a person into water. If they floated they were considered a witch. If they sank they were innocent. It was rather a no-win situation. Some witchhunters thought birthmarks were places where witches had fed their imps with their own blood. In Scotland torture was used to make people sign **confessions** – then they were executed. In England, though, torture was not used and far fewer people confessed to being witches.

THE END OF THE WITCHHUNTS

In England no witches were executed after 1682. In 1736 the law against witches was **repealed**. In Scotland there was a great witchhunt in 1661 and the last witch was executed in 1722. In 1751 an old Englishwoman, living at Tring, in Hertfordshire, was accused of being a witch and made to undergo the 'swimming test'. She died and one of the men who forced her was executed for murder. Things had changed since the days of Matthew Hopkins – but why?

WHY DID THE WITCHHUNTS END?

- England was more peaceful and people felt less frightened and insecure.
- There was less trouble between religious groups. Before this they had often accused each other of working for the devil.
- Changes in science meant that educated people stopped blaming natural problems on magic.
- Those educated people who were magistrates and judges treated witchhunters as lawless criminals.
- Many leading people disliked the violence and unrest caused by out-of-control witchhunts.

Altogether there were about 5,000 witchcraft trials in the British Isles between 1500 and 1730, and about 2,000 people were executed. In Germany there may have been as many as 90,000 trials and 20,000 executed in the same period of time.

Q

1. Look at **Source A**. Why was the 'swimming test' dangerous for a person accused of witchcraft, whichever way the test turned out?

2. In Scotland there were many more executions for witchcraft than in England. How might **Source B** help explain this?

3. It is the year 1751. Imagine a conversation between two people. One is the person accused of the murder of Ruth Osborne at Tring. The other is the judge. Imagine what they might say to each other. One will explain why he believes in witches. The other will say why he does not.

4. Look at **Sources C** and **D** and any other evidence. Explain why the great witchhunts finally came to an end.

Bring out your dead!

YOUR MISSION: to advise the Lord Mayor of London on how to fight the plague!

NEW WORDS

FASTING: not eating, to show how much you mean your prayers.

GENERATE: make something grow.

In 1665 a terrible cry echoed down the deserted London alleyways: 'Bring out your dead ... bring out your dead ...' The plague had returned. It was Bubonic Plague – a disease that had first appeared in Britain in 1348, over three hundred years earlier. Then it had been called the Black Death and over the three centuries since 1348 it had returned again and again.

The outbreak, in 1665, in London was the worst attack of the disease that had occurred in the capital in three hundred years. Out of a population of about 400,000, about 65,000 died. It raged through the summer and only declined as the cold of winter started. It was the last great outbreak of this killer disease in London.

'Ring, a ring o' roses' is a 17th-century plague song. The 'posies' were flowers thought to keep plague away, the 'roses' were red marks on the skin, the sneezing was a sign of plague.

SOURCE A

We whose names are attached do hereby at the request of the carrier of this letter, Mary Walker, certify that Mary and her master's whole family and all the neighbouring inhabitants are, and by God's blessing have been all summer, free from being visited with the plague.

▲ *A 'certificate of health'. It allowed the person who owned it to travel and leave London.*

SOURCE B

▲ *A 17th-century picture showing people running away from the plague. But they just take it with them (the skeletons) and cannot escape death.*

SOURCE C

A star or comet appeared for several months before the plague. The old women remarked that those two comets passed directly over the city and caused something strange to happen. The government decided on public prayers and days of **fasting** to make public confessions of sin and beg the mercy of God to stop the dreadful judgement.

The disaster was spread by infection, by the breath, by the sweat or by the stench of the sores of the sick people, or some other way. Some say it is carried in the air, which carries vast numbers of insects or invisible creatures, who enter into the body with the breath, or at the pores with the air and there **generate** most deadly poisons, or poisonous eggs, which mix with the blood and so infect the body.

▲ *Written by Daniel Defoe in* Journal of a Plague Year. *Defoe wrote about fifty years after 1665, but based his book on lots of evidence from the time.*

SOURCE D

August 12th. So many people die, that now they carry the dead to be buried by daylight, the nights not being long enough to do it in. The Lord Mayor commands people to be inside by 9 [pm] so that after that the sick will be free to go out for air.

▲ *From the* Diary *of Samuel Pepys, a wealthy citizen of London in 1665. Houses where plague appeared were locked, and those who lived there, not allowed to leave.*

Some people thought stray dogs carried the plague around the city. Dog killers were paid two pennies for every dog that they killed.

SOURCE E

Carts full of dead to bury.

▲ *A picture from the time showing victims of the plague being buried in pits outside the city of London.*

INVESTIGATION

You are the investigator!

Imagine that it is 1665 and the Lord Mayor of London has asked you to advise him how to fight the plague.

- Explain different theories of the cause of the plague;

- Explain why it is hard to run away and suggest ways that healthy people might be allowed to travel;
- What will you do to stop disease spreading?
- How will you cope with all the bodies?

11 ALL CHANGE

THE BIG PICTURE

THIS CHAPTER ASKS

What changes occurred in the way Britain was ruled after 1660?

Why did the Hanoverian royal family replace the Stuarts as rulers of Britain?

What differences did this make?

Were the victors at Culloden 'war ciminals'?

George II was the last British king to lead soldiers into battle, at Dettingen in Germany, in 1743. He won.

THE 'GLORIOUS REVOLUTION'

In 1660 Charles II returned as king. This is known as the '**Restoration**'. From then, until 1714, the Stuarts continued to rule Britain. In 1688, though, there was a great change, when James II was overthrown. James was brother to Charles II and became king when Charles died in 1685. At the end of his life Charles was turning towards Catholic beliefs and it was well known that James was a Catholic. This was a problem because many powerful people in Parliament and the majority of English people were against Catholicism. James made things worse for himself by trying to rule without Parliament and by trying to encourage Catholic beliefs. Many feared that if he could he would make Britain a Catholic country again. To protect himself he made Catholics officers in the army. This was all very unpopular and a group of leading men invited James's daughter, Mary, and her Dutch husband, William, to take the throne. James realised that few people supported him. He escaped to France and was replaced by William and Mary. This became known as the 'Glorious Revolution'.

PARLIAMENTS AND PROTESTANTS

All of this increased the power of Parliament. When William was offered the throne he had to agree to the Declaration of Rights (1689). This insisted that no taxes could be collected, or army gathered, without the agreement of Parliament. Parliament would be freely elected and would meet frequently; no Catholic could ever rule Britain.

In 1694, Queen Mary died; William had no children to succeed him. The next in line was Anne, Mary's sister, but she had no living children. Who would rule after Anne? The answer came in a law in 1701, called the Act of Settlement. This decided that the nearest Protestant relative was Princess Sophia, the granddaughter of James I. The crown would go to her, or her children.

William died in 1702 and Anne died in 1714. By this time Princess Sophia was dead and the new ruler of England was her son, the 54-year-old George I, Elector (ruler) of Hanover in Germany. In France, the son and grandson of the exiled James II plotted to replace him. Their supporters were the *Jacobites*.

Who were the Hanoverians?

George I: 1714–27   *George II: 1727–60*   *George III: 1760–1820*   *George IV: 1820–30*   *William IV: 1830–*

SCOTLAND AND ENGLAND

During Anne's reign the two countries were finally united. Ever since the Scot, James VI had become James I of England, in 1603, the two countries had been ruled by the same monarch but had separate Parliaments and ways of government. In 1707 the two Parliaments were replaced by one in London. The new country became known as the *United Kingdom of Great Britain*. Scotland did well out of the union but in the Highlands many of the clans disliked the English and, after 1714, their new German king. A lot of the English disliked him too! When there were Jacobite revolts, in 1715 and 1745, much of their support came from the Scottish Highlands. The revolts failed.

NEW WORDS

HANOVERIANS: the name given to the rulers of Britain from 1714-1837. They were kings of Britain and rulers of Hanover in Germany.
RESTORATION: to put something back. In this case, the Stuarts back as rulers.

How did the Hanoverians change the way Britain was governed?

George I spoke no English. He relied on his Ministers to control the government for him. The very first Prime Minister was Robert Walpole.

Rival parties in Parliament. 'Whigs' supported George and wanted a strong Parliament. 'Tories' wanted a strong king and some were Jacobites.

Jacobite Revolts in 1715 and 1745 against the Hanoverians.

English money and soldiers used to fight in European quarrels. This had started with William III.

Q

1. Explain how the Declaration of Rights, the Act of Settlement, and the Union with Scotland affected the way Britain was ruled.

2. In your own words explain the impact that the Hanoverians' becoming rulers had on the way Britain was governed.

Discussion Point
Do you think that it matters what a ruler's religious beliefs are? Give reasons for your answer.

'Hero' or 'war criminal'?

YOUR MISSION: to decide whether the Duke of Cumberland was responsible for the terrible crimes carried out after the Battle of Culloden, 1745.

In 1745 Charles Edward Stuart (the *'Bonnie Prince Charlie'* of Scottish legends) landed in Scotland. He was the grandson of James II and aimed to overthrow George II and put the Catholic Stuarts back on the British throne. The attempt was poorly organised, badly led and, despite the bravery of his Highland supporters which carried him as far south as the English city of Derby, it finally ended in his defeat at the Battle of Culloden, on 16 April 1746.

After the battle the soldiers of King George behaved with great cruelty towards their defeated and helpless Scottish enemies and towards many innocent people. We call such cruelties 'war crimes'. The commander of the **Royal** army was the son of George II, the Duke of Cumberland. Were these war crimes the responsibility of his soldiers? Or was the Duke himself a war criminal?

NEW WORDS

MANGLED: chopped and mixed up.

MUTILATED: smashed and chopped up.

ROYAL: supporters of George II. The Jacobites hoped to take the throne from King George.

SOURCE A

Along the road to Inverness I found twelve, or fourteen, bodies. Not all of them were Rebel soldiers. They had been stripped and **mutilated**. Close to Inverness I saw a boy of twelve lying with his head split to his teeth.

▲ *Actions of Royal soldiers after the battle. Written by an eyewitness.*

SOURCE B

Old Leanach Cottage. In the barn here, English soldiers burnt thirty rebels alive.

SOURCE C

In the rubbish were the bodies of several of those who had been burnt to death in a most miserable, **mangled** way.

▲ *Described by the eyewitness Mrs Taylor. The Royal soldiers had discovered wounded rebels in a hut, locked them in and burnt them to death.*

SOURCE D

They filled all the gaols in Inverness with rebel prisoners, wounded and naked. They ordered that no one should be allowed in to them with food or drink for two days. The wounded rotting in their gore and blood; some dead bodies covered with piss and dirt.

▲ *Written by John Farquharson, a rebel who survived.*

SOURCE E

We are carrying fire and destruction as we pass, shooting Highlanders we meet in the mountains and driving off the cattle.

▲ *A letter written by a Royal officer to the* London Magazine, *1746. Cumberland ordered that all goods and cattle taken were given to his soldiers.*

SOURCE F

Kill the insolent rebel.

▲ *Order given by Cumberland to one of his officers, Major Wolfe, about a badly wounded and defenceless rebel. But some versions say this was said by the Royal general Hawley.*

SOURCE I

Laws? I'll make soldiers give the laws!

▲ *Cumberland's reply to a Scottish leader who suggested he show mercy in carrying out the law against rebels.*

After Culloden, playing the bagpipes was declared to be an act of war. A Highland bagpiper was executed at York in 1746.

SOURCE G

March to all the cottages near the battlefield and search for rebels. The officers and men should remember that the public order of the rebels yesterday was to show us no mercy.

▲ *Cumberland's order to his soldiers. The rebels had not promised to show no mercy but Cumberland deliberately pretended they had.*

SOURCE J

All Scots are traitors and rebels like yourself.

▲ *Said by an English officer as he stabbed a dead rebel who had just been hanged.*

SOURCE H

In the Town House they were making out orders about the killing of the wounded left on the battlefield.

▲ *An eyewitness report about the Royal generals Hawley and Huske on the evening after the battle*

SOURCE K

These soldiers were drowned by the rebels after having been made prisoner. Rebel prisoners brought in that day were put by the well to see their own cruelty.

▲ *A letter written by an English officer about the rotting bodies of English soldiers found dumped in a well at Fort Augustus which the rebels had destroyed. This discovery happened over a month after the battle.*

INVESTIGATION

You are the investigator!

You are a war crimes investigator working for the International War Crimes Tribunal. Is the Duke of Cumberland guilty of war crimes?

- Were crimes committed? Explain your thinking.
- Identify the different kinds of crimes committed; who the victims were; who committed the crimes.
- What evidence is there that officers other than the Duke of Cumberland may have been responsible for ordering these crimes?
- What evidence links Cumberland to the crimes?

How responsible do you think Cumberland was?

THE BIG PICTURE

INTO THE MODERN WORLD

Britain in 1750 was at the beginning of the modern world. The British were victorious in wars against their old rivals, the French, and were starting to win an Empire abroad, in America and India. At home, the population was rising quickly and farmers and inventors were experimenting with new ways to meet the growing demand for food, cotton and woollen clothes, and other goods. What would one day be called the *Agricultural* and *Industrial Revolutions* were starting. John Wesley – the founder of Methodism – was stirring up the country as he preached about Jesus in the roughest and toughest areas of British towns and cities. Britain had come a long way from the end of the Middle Ages in 1500.

> There are new ideas in farming, new inventions in the cotton cloth industry. One day these inventions will change the world.

Inventor

Welsh

> We have the same rights as the English now. Richer Welshmen can become judges, MPs, courtiers, merchants.

> We are a Protestant country now. The Church of England doesn't want to share power with any other Christian groups.

Churchman

> Elizabeth, Cromwell and William III crushed our rebellions. Our land has been given to Protestant settlers. Catholics are second-class citizens in their own land.

Irish

> The country's changing. We are making money out of better farming and investing it in new industries.

Nobleman

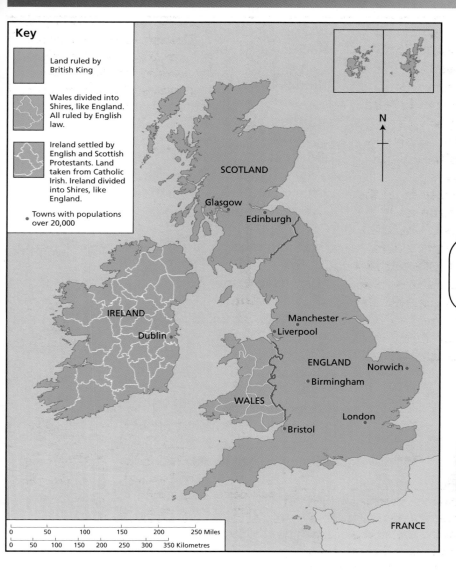

Key

Land ruled by British King

Wales divided into Shires, like England. All ruled by English law.

Ireland settled by English and Scottish Protestants. Land taken from Catholic Irish. Ireland divided into Shires, like England.

Towns with populations over 20,000

SCOTLAND

Glasgow

Edinburgh

IRELAND

Dublin

Manchester

Liverpool

ENGLAND

Norwich

Birmingham

WALES

London

Bristol

FRANCE

N

| 0 | 50 | 100 | 150 | 200 | 250 Miles |
| 0 | 50 | 100 | 150 | 200 | 250 | 300 | 350 Kilometres |

We've done well from the Union. We can share English trade in the growing Empire, but we resent losing control of our country.

Scot

No one can ignore Parliament. Rulers can't govern without our support.

Member of Parliament

The Christian preacher, John Wesley, rode over 250,000 miles on horseback to preach about Jesus.

Q **1.** Look back at the first BIG PICTURE and compare it with this one. Choose six ways in which Britain changed between 1500 and 1750 and write these down, so that you could share them with a neighbour, or your class.

2. Look at all the ways in which Britain changed between 1500 and 1750. Which change do you think was the most important? Explain why.

Index